THE MORAY WAY

And introducing the

BEN MACDUI TRAIL

D1744640

Paul Carpenter

Published by Lulu.com

ISBN 978-1-4478-8568-9

Other publications by Paul Carpenter

Travel;

Six Mountain hikes from around the World

Crafts;

Leather and Wood Crafts

The leather lace Bullwhip

Leather Armour

Leather Projects

Archers Craft

Copyright © 2011 Paul Carpenter

www.mtn-m.co.uk

All telephone numbers, web addresses correct as of 2011. The Author has made every effort to ensure historical dates, events and names are correct, but in the unlikely hood that any are found to be wrong please inform him at info@mtn-m.co.uk

Front cover image – Elgin Cathedral at sunset

Back cover painting of Author by Robert Blackwell, a local artist from Forres - http://www.facebook.com/#!/pages/Robert-Blackwell-Artist/206245722719472

To Jack and Mitch

CONTENTS

THE MORAY WAY – THE DETAILS

THE BEN MACDUI TRAIL – THE DETAILS

INTRODUCTION

Moray, Oh Moray so good they only had to name it once. Its small it's compact, it's a wonderland full of surprises;

- M – has to stand for the **M**ountains, some of the highest in the UK where myth and mother nature still kick a…

- O – for **O**h my god look at the size of that Salmon that you might be lucky enough to catch or see jumping.

- R – **R**obert Burns and his quote 'Freedom an whisky gang thegither' and with over 15 distilleries in Moray (once thousands of illicit ones) you can just taste the freedom.

- A – for **A**ir and amongst the freshest on this grand Isle, just ask the old man beard dripping off of the birch.

- Y – Considering the four above it has to mean, wh**Y** the heck haven't you considered coming here before!

So what is so special about Moray that should impel you to drop everything (after reading this book) and head for it as if your life depended on it? To help make this blatantly clear let us start at one of its high points, this being Ben Avon grid reference NJ132019.

To the west of this high ground stands the mass of Cairngorms plateau holding sway to the furthermost tip of Morays county boundary. Turning north it is possible from this vantage point on a clear day to see the calamities, natural and manmade which transformed this land into what is seen today as before you rolls out a view over the lower hills leading to the low fertile lands (Known as the 'Laich o' Moray') and finally the coast.

About 12,000 years ago, this peak would have been covered in a mighty glacier and would have been the last place you would want to stand, knee deep in solid ice whose awesome mechanical movements grinded away at everything in its path helping to create the huge corries now seen along the Lairig Ghru. Luckily, the glaciers started to melt just in time to allow the earth to warm up enough to give us these nice summers we have today! The torrent of melted water swept down the easiest gradient opening up avenues to the coast beyond the lower hills depositing huge amounts of sediment starting the process of creating excellent farm land plus the odd hummock to build quaint little castles, churches and forts on, just waiting for the early settlers to arrive.

However, that was not until about 3,000 BC, before the arrival of man woodland and forest developed fast on the footsteps of the glaciers. Huge expanses of not just pine but great oak grew covering the whole area in a nice warm blanket of needles and leaf, which was called the Atlantic forest or more commonly the Caledonian Forest, bringing along with it the large animals that used to roam here such as the bear and wolf.

Once this excellent housing material had matured and the abundance of food supply had settled, along with the great salmon finding a few more rivers to struggle up. Then the haphazard groups of pre-historic people wandered this way pushed further up north by groups down south starting the process of civilizing the land by colonizing areas close to food and which offer the best protection. Hence, the first settlement were created, namely Burghead with its nice outcrop of rock surrounded by an inland marshy loch not far from the fertile flatlands around Forres, which also had or still does a perfect high hill for lookouts.

Over the proceeding thousands of years these people developed a severe hatred of the midge along with a few tools, starting with the humble cracked rock then later a dark hard substance, which could be moulded into all sorts of things. With this, these people developed into an isolated (due to the mountain barriers) organized group governed and taxed just we are today, but who had a fascination for painting their faces blue.

These were the Picts or Caledonians, who the Romans, despite holding sway over the rest of the UK for 3 centuries, could not bring to heel. Going by the many coin hordes found locally, they preferred to bribe for peace while they went about their business wearing shiny armour, starting the concept of paved roads and eating exotic food while watching warriors kill each other.

After the Romans left, the Vikings came and stayed, and the period of political unrest, battles, ownership, religious and royalty turmoil began serving ever more to produce that one great item. The castle ruin, which provides so much entertainment these days plus the unfortunate demise of the great Caledonian forest eaten up by the blood thirst and history of human naval conflict, as well as some bits, cleared for farming.

In amongst all of this is what makes this place so special. One obviously being the natural forces that have and will constantly change this landscape but most importantly it is the little folk, the lads, lassies, loons and lairds. Around their hard work and good humour has developed a land full of history and intrigue, of its clans and their fight for freedom, all accomplished without the aid of mobile phones and microwaves. They grew a legacy started by their ancestors as they defied English rule and later not paying tax on illicit whisky, whose huge boat fleets from harbours large and small, brought supplies from around the world and whose rivers supply two of the world's great luxuries; the dram and salmon steak.

To see, feel and experience what is best of Moray, these routes within this book are as good a start as any at giving you the opportunity to meet the small folk, and sample the delicacies produced here, such as whisky, salmon and Cullen skink. Depending on the time of year, you may even be lucky enough to leave with the same if not worse hatred of all the dreaded midges!

HOW TO GET THE BEST FROM THIS BOOK

All of the information sections are self-explanatory about what they contain. i.e. If you need to know how to poo in the woods, then there's a whole page about it with diagrams, plus the same for bikes and boots, but you may be wandering about the main sections called 'The basics' and 'The detail'.

These were created to cater for three types of reader;

The Basic's – For those of us who just want the nitty gritty fact and figures, who just need to know the essentials and are off like a bat out of a cave.

The Details – This is a much larger section written for the gentler, serene types who just love to find out about an areas colourful and even violent historical bits and pieces and take their time doing it.

Both The Basics and Details – No harm in reading both sections and is ideal for the inbetweeners who would use the basics first to get an idea of the trails and then read the detail when they are bored or laying exhausted in the B and B.

The Routes within this book are purposely not set out in durations of day 1 and day 2 type but rather set out in sections because everybody has their own pace be it on foot or on a bike. Moreover they can, from the simple maps provided, assert for themselves how far they would like to go and choose where to stay the night? This is after all supposed to be fun not a test of endurance and, if you want to spend the occasional lunch sipping the odd dram – go ahead!

How not to get lost – Grid Refs and Bearings

Some people may say that the best way to find your way around is to literally "get lost" when in a new town or area. It certainly makes you more aware of your surroundings and can be quite good fun at times where you're more likely to register and remember such things as landmarks, street names, takeaways in a hope that your remember them later on and may even give you a better understanding of the lay of the land over time.

By foot or on bike through the countryside on routes such as those within this book, there is no time nor is it safe to use this getting lost method. It's better to know where you're going before hand and this is where maps come in handy, which contain a wealth of information about a location if read properly, and should definitely be carried along with a compass during any hiking trip.

There are whole books devoted on the subject of reading maps and using compass, which should be referred to if, you have no or little knowledge on the subject. Only the basics of how not to get lost are shown within this one to hopefully keep you on the right paths.

Grid Reference

First off are **grid references**. All maps have a square grid super imposed over them whose primary purpose is to enable an area or place to be pinpointed by the numbers on each of the lines that make up the grid. The vertical lines or 'Easting's' are numbered from west to east and the horizontal lines or 'Northing's' are numbered from south to north as shown in fig1.

Irrespective of the scale of a map, each square made up within the grid represents 1km on the ground, thus, when you get a four-digit grid reference; it is only accurate to $1km^2$. To get a greater degree of accuracy you use a 6-digit grid reference, which is accurate to within $100m^2$.

For most purposes, a **6-digit grid reference** is given along with the OS map sheet number.

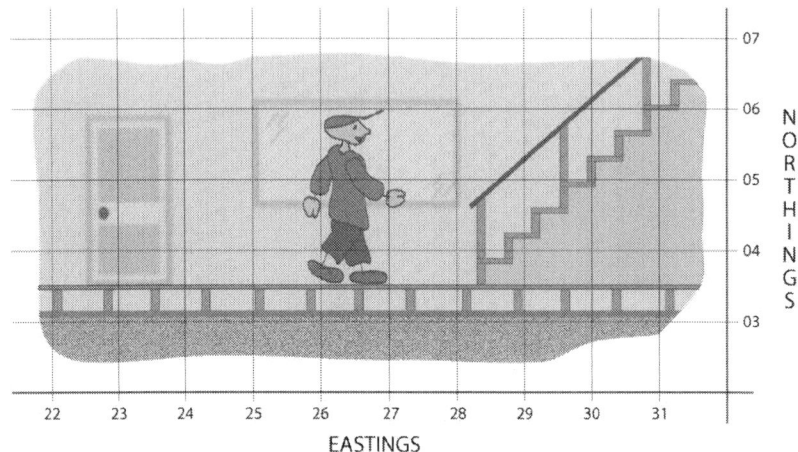

Figure 1 – along the corridor and up the stairs

As with most things there is a certain way to read the grid numbers, and fig 1 helps to explain this; the saying which comes to mind to help remember the right numbers to read first is 'along the corridor and up the stairs' i.e. the easting's are read first and then the northing's.

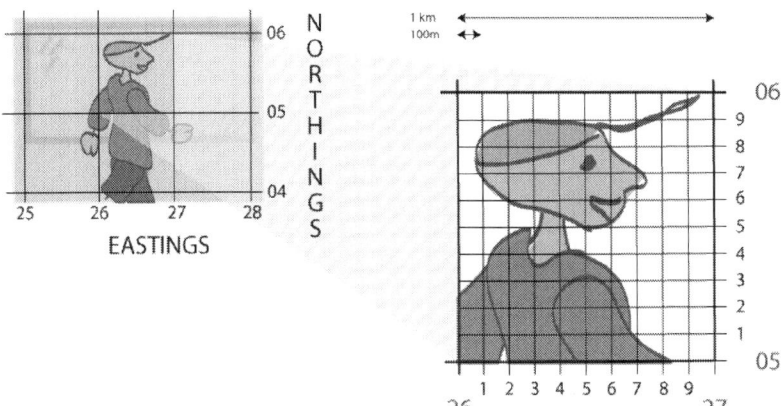

Figure 2 – 6 figure grid reference

For this example, we are going to pinpoint the position of the cartoon characters eye. Initially you need to give the grid reference (four-digit number) of the square containing the eye. This would be grid reference 2605 – 26 being the Easting's and 05 being the Northing's.

Fig 2 shows this grid square 2605 isolated and blown up to reveal how each square is further divided into smaller squares, each being 100m². These smaller squares are not shown on a map but rather you have to either use the Romar scales as shown in fig 3 or do your best guess if you don't have your compass to hand.

Now using the Romar scale or best guess you can give a six digit number of the characters eye. This being grid reference 265057 – always ensuring that you state all the easting's number first before the northing's.

Sheet number or Grid squares

Normally when a grid reference is given, you are told beforehand from which OS sheet number it belongs to i.e. OS sheet 36, or the grid reference merely has two letters before it i.e. NC265057, these referring to a grid square within the grid system covering the UK.

You will need one or the other because the numbers, which run along the Easting and Northing's lines, only go from 0 to 99, thus are repeated every 100km meaning that a 6 figure grid reference from one area could be the same as from another.

If given the sheet number then it is just a simple matter of ensuring what your using that sheet and for local searches i.e. less than 100km square the letters are not be needed. If however you are using software such as OS getamap, which would enable a countrywide search then the letters should be used – on any sheet these are highlighted where 0 or 99 appear along the grid lines.

All grid reference within this book are given with grid letters.

Bearings

Grid references are good to find where a place is but they don't really aid you in finding your way there, and this is where **bearings** come into play.

A **Bearing** is basically a value from 0 to 360 degrees, which acts like imagining a clock around your feet i.e. if you wanted someone to look left, you'd say anywhere between 07.00 to 11.00 o'clock depending on the severity of the turn needed. Except with bearings they align with the points of the compass i.e. south is 180 degrees, east is 90 degrees etc and not as with the clock, where no matter which direction you are facing, straight ahead is always 12.00.

There is a lot more to bearings, which can be studied elsewhere, for the purposes of this book you only need to know how to get/read a bearing and walk on it.

As mentioned a bearing is a good device to use to keep you in the right direction, sometimes it is handy when organizing a trip to take these bearings along your route between prominent features while at home to avoid using the map while out of the wind or rain. But sometimes changes in routes demand you do it during the trip.

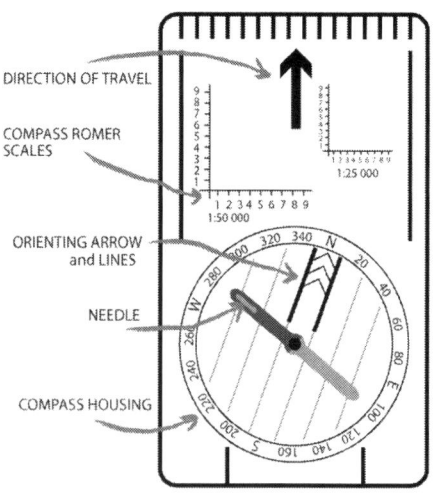

Figure 3 – Parts of a compass

In some instances, especially when navigating around lowlands when you are surrounded by many obstacles such as woods, hills, buildings etc , you cannot see your objective like you can (when weather permits) up on mountains. It tends to be a big disadvantage to head straight for a destination as in all probability you will not arrive exactly on target and either walk past it or if, heading for the house as in fig 4, may get to the road and not know which direction the house is in. The trick to use in these instances is to **aim off** of your destination to either side, thus when you arrive at the road, you will definitely know which direction the house is in.

Always remember to ensure that the route you plan to take does not take you over dangerous or difficult to cross obstacles such as over cliffs when in the mountains or as shown in fig 4, not across the river where a crossing could be dangerous – where possible use paths and bridges.

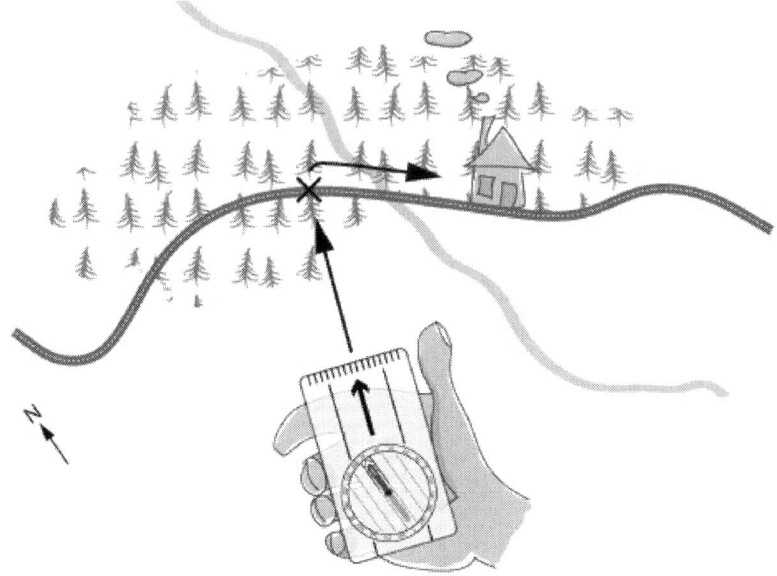

Figure 4 – using aiming off for bearing on ground

Getting a bearing on the ground – using fig 4 as the example,

- Point the 'direction of travel' arrow on the compass in the direction you wish to go.

- Turn the compass housing until the north end of the needle is aligned with orientating arrow and lines.

- Note the bearing and follow ensuring you periodically check that the needle is still aligned with the orientating lines.

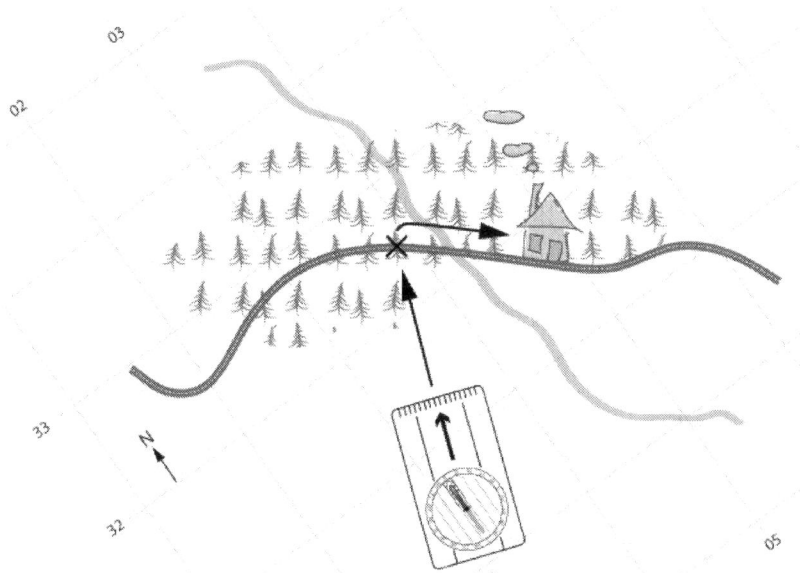

Figure 5 – using aiming off for bearing from map

Getting a grid bearing from a map – using fig 5 as an example.

- Align the compass in the direction you wish to travel from your present location on the map.

- Turn the compass housing until the orientating arrow and lines are in line with the map grid lines running north.

- Hold compass and turn until the north of the needle is in line with the orientating arrow and lines.

- Note the bearing and follow as before checking periodically that you are heading in the right direction.

You may have heard of the old synonym involving bearings;

Grid to Mag – add

Mag to Grid – get rid

These refer to the difference in degrees between magnetic north (direction the compass needle points) and grid north (direction the map northing gridlines point), when on occasion you take a bearing from the ground (Mag) and wish to transfer it to the map (grid), you have to subtract this difference from your bearing to get the correct bearing. Plus visa versa when getting a bearing from the map to use on the ground, you have to add this difference.

Over very short distances these changes may not be necessary or when using 'aiming off' but definitely if near or around dangerous features such as cliffs.

The amount you need to add or subtract changes over time and is stated on all maps along with an annual change either along the top of the map or within the information section.

Using due east as an example of the measure of a bearing, $90°00'$ is made up of

- $90°$ (hours)

- $00'$ (minutes)

A map will state the difference at the time of printing, for example; $05°25'$ with an annual change of $45'$. If the map being used was for example 5 years old, then this would mean a total of $09°10'$ being added or subtracted from a bearing (remembering that one hour or 1 degree contains 60 minutes just like on a clock).

- $45' \times 5$ (years) $= 225' \div 60 = 3.75$ or $03°45'$

- $03°45' + 05°25' = 09°10'$

BIKE AND BOOTS

Before delving into the basic's and advise of which and what to use, (in the authors opinion) it would be prudent to say that to cover these routes you could forgo the energetic methods of transport in preference to more laid back and serene means of forward motion by employing the humble car, motorbike or even by hoof.

This would be especially possible around the The Moray Way where the majority of the route and tourist hot spots around it are near to roads and settlements. For horses, the Dava way section has been especially modified with them in mind. Alas, for the majority of the Ben Macdui Trail, bike or boots are definitely required.

However, let us face it; you want to dive straight into the beauty and majestic scenery of Moray and not miss a single gem and for that you will have to get those legs moving. Your choice of whether it is by bike or boots is up to you but to aid this decision the author took bike and boots along both routes, with the exception of the stage from Ford of Avon to Ben Macdui. Which in his opinion you'd have to be either insanely fit or off your head to want to carry the bike that far. In essence, he was daft enough to cover every inch of these routes the hard way so that you would not have to!

- **Bike** – Going by bike will mean you cover more ground and go a lot faster (especially downhill), and will probably be more appropriate to those addicted to pedal power or which have a narrow time window in which to complete all or parts of the routes.

Figure 6 - front suspension road/touring bike or Duel suspension mountain bike?

- Choice of Bike – For The Moray way you could get away with a road bike if you choose to avoid all the rougher parts of the trail but in general a mountain bike will be needed. For the Ben Macdui trail you may need a much more technical mountain bike for using after Tomintoul, but remember that dual suspension bikes cannot take panniers - both should; have had a recent service, and be cleaned after every day if travelling over boggy ground - the last thing you need is a brake seizure downhill! But even if the bike is hired checking all cables, brake pads, bolts and screws might be advisable.

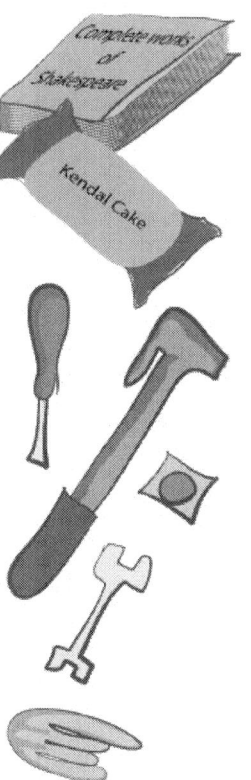

Having quick release bolts on both wheels it quite handy for those odd occasions when you get punctures along the road.

Items which should be carried and worn include helmet, spare inner tube, pump, reflective vest (for road use) and basic tools allowing for basic road side repairs.

- Skills – The workings of a bike, be it expensive or cheap are fairly similar and simple. As long as you know how to use spanners, screwdrivers and Allen keys, no disaster should be too drastic for you to handle. If on the other hand they should, then perhaps you need to learn about the basic workings of a bike and at least how to repair some faults such as a puncture before venturing out into the void, while also picking up some basic road and off road riding skills along the way.

If hiring a bike, the shop should be able to give some advice about the more technical riding skills, Glenmore lodge now holds courses in this. Please see page 19 for contacts.

- **Boots** – Using this method obviously shows a willingness to take longer where you may only want to cover bits at a time while carrying a light day sack or carry a heavier load needed for overnight camps while covering the whole or larger sections.

  There is a lot to think about when considering long distance trails, which these two are, especially for those unaccustomed to constant footwork. But the rewards in the author's opinion offer a far greater intimacy with your surroundings than pedal power would, plus as the author found it is a heck of a lot easier to walk over boggy and rocky ground without a bike in tow!

- Choice of Boots – The best choice of boots does differ for every individual and should be researched properly especially if you are not used to long walks. Unfortunately, the flood of hiking or walking boots out there in shopping land does not help in trying to pick the right item to keep your most important asset safe and happy – that is your feet!

-

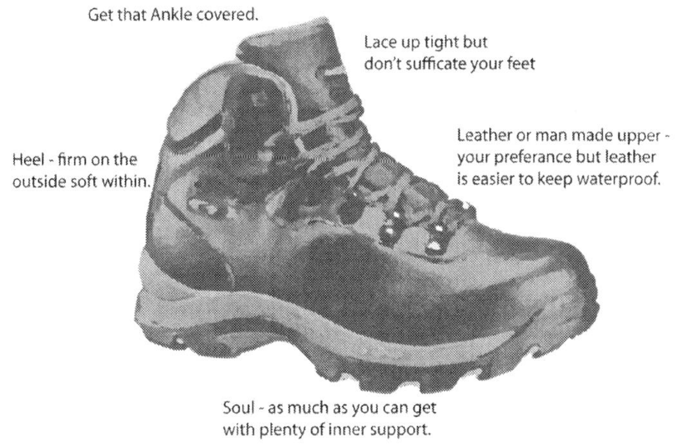

Get that Ankle covered.

Lace up tight but don't sufficate your feet

Leather or man made upper - your preferance but leather is easier to keep waterproof.

Heel - firm on the outside soft within.

Soul - as much as you can get with plenty of inner support.

Figure 7 - Aspects of a Boot

In the Author's 30 plus years of stomping around all over the place, he has found that the best advice is to forget the newest shiny gadget and spring loaded boot. Rather try and pick something that is close to or of the same make to what you are used to wearing for everyday use i.e. if you're used to soft flexible shoes, don't try stiff solid soled boots, your just end up with blisters. Also, try to use cotton hiking socks as these tend to be the best at absorbing sweat and stop the rubbing which is the cause of most blisters – if you are the sort who get blisters all the time regardless, the compeed blister patches work wonders!

- Skills – As in the technical stuff, this is dealt with elsewhere in this book, the skills referred to here are those of walking, plain and simple – yes that thing you've been doing since about 6 months old. Except the walking you have done since then has thanks to countless road workers been done on smooth even surfaces including road running.

During these routes you will find yourself walking over a variety of surfaces, none of which could be described as smooth and even like tarmac, rather more like stones, boggy, and soft sand. All of which will cause you to use more energy than you normally would over tarmac and push your foot all around the boot, hence the rubbing!

For short day trips, this might not be an issue but for longer periods, it could be and should be considered along with your general fitness and how you go about keeping fit. Maybe try some cross-country running or just walking over rough land now and again.

BIKES AND BOOTS - Providers

http://www.halfords.com/
Lossie Wynd, Elgin, 01343 552030
For cycle sales, spare parts and servicing.

http://stuartscycles.co.uk/
32 High Street, Forres, 01309 672432
For cycle sales/rentals, parts and servicing.

http://www.mortimersofspeyside.co.uk/
3 High Street, Grantown on Spey, 01479 872684
For outdoor clothing and fishing tackle

http://www.millets.co.uk/home.html
Unit 13, St Giles centre, 01343 556550
For outdoor clothing, boots and equipment.

http://speysiderunner.com/
59 High Street, Fochabers, 01343 821377
Specializes in sport gear for runners.

Ross Outdoors Ltd
125 High Street, Nairn, 10667 454900
Offers outdoor and climbing equipement.

POO'S IN THE WILD

Poo's, more commonly referred to by a four letter word spoken out loud in haste when something goes wrong, or in some instances referred to as 'sugar' despite not having the same punch! But why oh why is there a section on excrement when perhaps the non-persistent aromas of flatulence are of more concern and the availability of toilets and nearness of settlements to the trails in this book might not make it a concern.

Unfortunately, as you walk around these trails you might be unfortunate to see the reason in the form of helpings of bangers and mash at the side of the path (the mash of course being toilet paper). Then of course, there are the recent warnings posted at the Faindouran Lodge on approach to the River Avon ford where improper dumping of human waste has caused a case of food poisoning.

Now on the defense of the poo'ee it is not always possible to spend time taking care in the placement of said waste, especially when exposing possibly the fairest, softest and whitest part of the body to the extreme windy, wet and cold environments of the Cairngorms upon a typical summer's day.

All the same, the bad side to the Cairngorms getting the recognition it deserves and being stated as one of the top 10 locations of the world (National Geographic) will undoubtedly mean an increase in possible miss-placed Poo's. It is not possible to say turn the urge to poo off as any doctor would say this is not healthy and naturally you will be eating high energy and rich food to supplement the increase in exertion. In the end when you got to go, you got to go.

The only solution would seem to be that as an individual or group, you will have to add one small item to your kit list, namely something like a garden trowel with which to dig a small or large hole depending on length of stay and amount of possible users. It's no use crying 'but sheep, cows and deer poo all over the place, why should I have to get down and dirty' simply put they eat from the system and poo into the system, they are part of the local food chain, we are not and thus cannot just cock a leg and dump. Below are a few suggestions of methods of pooing in the wilds that could be used by individuals, groups and even establishments.

- The Multi-single use poo dispenser – With said trowel or shovel if provided, this is ideal for an individual or groups of up to 4 to use staying in the same location for one or two nights.

Once you have arrived at your chosen night location, recce out a place away from rivers, streams, buildings and paths on a flat area, if possible out of the wind and allowing some privacy.

Pull away stones and undergrowth such as heather, pine needles, grass until peat or soil is exposed and dig down about 1 1/2 foot depositing the waste around the edge of the hole (diameter of hole depending on size of your derrière).

Lastly place some stones around the diameter to allow for support and your multi-single use poo dispenser is ready, no longer requiring a potential desperate user to scramble about in the mountains, woods or moors.

On average only two people might use it, for groups of more the 4 build other ones and after each deposit cover said excrement and paper with some earth/peat ready for next user. The hole will probably fill with water so expect a splash or two.

As for the jug and barrel beautifully drawn within the earth of the picture – many roman coin hordes have been found in moray plus a lot of illicit whisky distillering happened in these parts, so you never know what you might dig up!

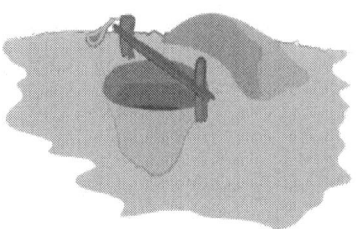

- Group Use – Could still be dug with a trowel but a shovel would be more appropriate in this instant. Also needed would be three lengths of timber or branches for the seat support.

For use by groups of up to 15 staying in the same location for more than 4 nights, more than likely permission would have to be granted from land owner for its use as well as the other activities which the group will do.

Recce out a position as discussed in previous example but this time after clearing area of debris, dig down to about waist height with a diameter of 2 to 3 feet depositing waste to one side. Next build support as shown in drawing just off centre and attach the trowel to one support to aid depositing soil into hole after each use. The hole will probably fill with water so expect a bigger splash or two.

- Semi-permanent use – Would involve a lot more construction and thus would probably be built by the owner or caretaker in an area/location where people frequently stay overnight or longer giving them a dry centralized location to dispose of their waste. Especially good where vehicle access is possible to wood, moor or mountain location.

Basically it is a large hole lined with stones, covered by a port-a-loo type building which when full is either piped off or burnt.

TICKS AND MIDGES

Apparently, the last wild carnivorous animal in Scotland, the wolf, was killed near to River Findhorn by a game stalker in 1743 unless of course you believe in the myths and folklore of the area and thus fear to see the black wolf or hear its bark, which heralded the approach of death himself.

But less of this playing around......there are still predators out there just waiting for you on the moors, woods and hills whose appetite for human blood makes the wolf look like sweet little puppies in comparison. Plus whose numbers and areas of affliction just seem to increase on a yearly basis.

It is the Ticks and infamous Midges of Scotland referred to here, those vampires and pains in almost every nook and cranny of your body that can turn a wonderful summer's sunset into mayhem, madness and a lot of swearing – it almost makes you wonder how the kilt clad high and lowlanders of old managed? Must have been a tough lot back then and now.

Now is also when you have to step up and face the mean beasties of Moray and here are a few methods, which have proved useful to disperse or alleviate their blood addictions in some instances, but sadly totally useless on other occasions as it is true, the strength of their bite does seem to alter from area to area.

Probably the worst of them are on the west coast, so a big sigh of relief can be excelled but they are closely followed by the Cairngorms near rivers followed next by Dava Moor in damp areas (which can mean most of it during wet spells).

Ticks

These are what could be technically called stealth jungle warriors who use guerilla tactics along with their small size and absence of irritation or pain to crawl all over you without you knowing.

They are crab like parasites which are mostly found in long grass and heather where live stock is kept and also where the wild deer roam, which pretty much means everywhere else!

In high summer, their numbers can be such that they are quite visible within high grass increasing the danger of attack if you venture off tracks and paths, this could be especially true on The Moray Way where certain parts cut through high banks.

Once they do land on you, they do not dig in straight away but would rather take their sweet time to find their favorite locations which are normally the hairy bits, but they will also equally do with nice smooth bits. So this gives you some time to periodically check your legs or arms and any other exposed parts and brush them off before they get a chance to refresh their selves.

Once dug in the main danger from these silent parasites would be to those more susceptible to Lyme's disease, an infectious disease which can produce symptoms similar to influenza.

To help prevent catching any of these sinister fellows the only thing you can do is cover all fleshy bits, so try to wear long trousers and periodically check yourself and any pets for ticks. Especially check pets before going into accommodation or a tent as if they are carrying some they may fall off only to go in search of easier prey.

When dug in, it is the head, which is under the skin with the larger body section exposed. Do not try to rub or twist them out as this will only cause the head to be left in giving you a larger chance of catching an infection. Use tweezers or long nails to grasp the tick as close to the skin as possible and pull out gently.

Because of their size and lack of irritation you may not even know that you have been bitten but if you develop symptoms later on like influenza i.e. headaches, muscle sores (if not from the exercise!) fever, then go see a doctor.

On the brighter side of things, apart from the infection bit and the sucking your blood habit, they are not that annoying, at least not as bad as our next topic is;

Midges

These can only be described as kamikaze brutes who just love to dive bomb in huge squadrons ensuring maximum depth as they stick their front cutter into you and even have the audacity to use histamines within their saliva to make your blood more palatable to them. Incidentally it is only the female which feeds on blood, the male being happier just to suck on nectar.

If they were not bad enough, there are also the larger mosquitoes and assortment of other blood suckers which can either join forces with the Midges or attack in their absence with the same gusto. Plus it seems the only people who can catch them in the air are martial arts experts, the rest of us just look like lunatics thrashing around.

Returning to the most notorious of them, the midges, it is this histamines which causes most of the bad after effects, from itchiness to full blown swelling up like a balloon, along with the ever present hordes diving and gliding around your head constantly without rest.

It seems that they are attracted to the CO_2 we excell, so to avoid them would be a simple matter of not breathing or wear a respirator and full body non breathable suit. Naturally this is not going to happen but they do seem to attack more when you are stationary, so just keep walking as they hate wind even that which is created while walking because it breaks their fragile wings…ah poor sweet little things!

Using smoke such as from a fire or from smokers to deter them is not that effective but smoke repellent coils do work. Drowning down loads of vitamin C or Garlic before hand in the hope that they don't like the taste of your sweat is also fairly unproductive; it just deters most people away from you.

Of the hordes of manmade repellents, there are two which seem to stand above the rest for cost and effectiveness, these being;

- Avon skin so soft spray – Despite the un-macho name this is used by soldiers of the armed forces and has many followers who just love putting their selves in harms way to test it.

  A disadvantage could be the fact that it is a spray and thus unless positioned next to the skin will act like wireless; everybody else will get it as well as you.

- Autan active stick – This is like a roll on and thus will give better coverage allowing you to apply as much or little needed depending on the approaching invasion.

I do hope that this short description of a few of Moray's beasties has not put you off venturing the beautiful by-ways. Just remember to cover up and slap the repellent on and get someone else to stop and take the scenic snap shots.

SAFETY NOTES AND GRADE KEY

The pretty little maps provided within this book are in no way a substitute for an OS map and are merely created to help indicate the positions of photos also provide a quick reference to places mentioned and give a general idea of the routes.

All distances and elevations for both routes are taken from GTX files created at OS get a map (www.getamap.ordnancesurveyleisure.co.uk/) which can be downloaded onto your GPS and are available for download from my freebies page (www.mtn-m.co.uk/freebies.html).

The grades are shown on the cautious side of safety normally illustrating the worst trail conditions along a certain stage based on the experiences of the author who is 40'ish of mid range fitness. i.e. not a superman, nor a couch potato but on average able to walk 12 miles in one day quite comfortably without severe muscle ache afterwards plus whose mountain biking experience extends mostly to forest trails and maintained mountain paths.

The trails within this book involve going from coastal paths to quaint safe forest trails leading to rocky exposed mountainous ones, so an awareness of and preparation for these extremes of dangers should be considered reference clothing, fitness, food, navigation, first aid. If you are for any reason unsure of your abilities or skills then either get trained or join one of the local guides listed on page 31..

If you are not part of an organized group then you should pick a responsible person to let someone know where you are going and likely to be back (B & B owners, relative etc), this could also include (especially out in the mountains) possible escape routes if the weather deteriates or a member of the group gets tired. It would also be a good idea to give your mobile numbers to these people but remember that although reception is good throughout Moray and on mountain tops, there is no or very little reception within the glens of Cairngorms and the WW2 Coastal Defences.

The route involved around The Moray Way is mostly close to roads except from Lossiemouth to Kingston, and if you decide to explore the caves from Clashach Cove to Covesea settlement you will get trapped when the tide is in. The Ben Macdui Trail involves entering into exposed and wilderness areas which in the later parts are far away from roads where the need to tell people where you are increases.

For this purpose, an example Route Card is shown in figure 8 outlining the route the author took from Tomintoul to Ben Macdui and the eventual changes he had to make due to the weather preventing him from covering the route as planned. Remember you can always return to these mountains as they are some of the oldest in the world and are not likely to disappear soon (despite the intense efforts of the clouds, wind, snow and ice). A PDF of this route card is available from my freebies page.

Note - when using Naismith's rule to calculate times, take into account your or that of the slowest persons fitness, Plus whoever is carrying the most gear.

One last aspect that should be brought up is accommodation. Around the Moray Way B & B's and Hotels abound, the same during the early stages of the Ben Macdui Trail, but after Tomintoul there is only the bothy or Faindouran Lodge at NJ082062 plus three mountain refuges within the Cairngorms. These being;

- The ford of Avon refuge at NJ041031.
- The Hutchinson memorial hut at NO022998 found just under Loch Etchachan.
- The Corrour bothy at NN981958 found under Devil Point in the Lairig Ghru.
- Plus some may include the shelter stone at the end of Loch Avon at NJ001016.

It should be noted that apart from the Lodge, all four of the refuges are not meant for overnight stays, but merely as 'Refuges' from bad weather. Despite this people do use them even while the insulation properties of some are similar to that of a paper towel in a blizzard. There used to be a lot more of these refuges throughout the Cairngorms but after an accident where a group of girls used one and perished, most were removed.

Unless you want the same to happen to you make sure that before using any of the bothys or refuges for overnight stays that you plan for it in your route card and are carrying the right gear.

The Moray Way

- 1:50 000 Landranger - numbers 27, 28, 36
- 1:25 000 Explorer   - numbers 418, 419, 423, 424

The Ben Macdui trail

- 1:50 000 Landranger - numbers 28, 36
- 1:25 000 Explorer   - numbers 403, 404, 419, 423

TRAINING/GUIDED TRIPS PROVIDERS

http://www.glenmorelodge.org.uk/

Glenmore lodge, Aviemore – need to brush up on your navigation, mountain biking, general or mountain walking skills, there is no better place than here.

http://www.contours.co.uk/index.htm

Offers walking holidays throughout the UK.

http://www.macsadventure.com/index.php

Offers Trips and expeditions by bike and hiking throughout the World.

http://www.easyways.com/

Offers accommodation booking service and hiking trails within Scotland.

http://www.cairngormmountain.co.uk/

Winter and summer website for attractions and walks within the Cairngorm Mountains.

http://www.wild-things.org.uk/

Offers wilderness, bushcraft, and nature experiences/training, and runs summer camps. Based in Findhorn.

http://www.wildatheart-ecoholidays.com/

Offer unique wildlife watching trips, nature retreats and family holidays, located in the stunning and unspoilt county of Moray.

Names in Group plus mobile numbers -		
Paul Carpenter		
Date *18/07/2001*	**Start location** *Tomintoul, argyle B and B.*	**Objective** *Ben Macdui then ski centre*
Distance (Mile/km) *30 miles*	**Maps used and time sunset** *OS sheet 36, 404, 403 – 21.50 hours*	

From *start location*	Route description	Height Gain/Distance	est time
To *Faindouran Lodge*	*Tarmac road to inchrory (179081) then gravel track to lodge (082062)*	*341m, 15.7 miles*	*5.5 hours*
To *Ben Macdui*	*Rocky paths and steep trails to summit via ford of Avon (042032) up to loch Avon – ascent steep path to plateau (006024) – head to Lochan buidhe (984011) then onto Ben Macdui (989989)*	*702m, 9.2 miles*	*4.2 hours*
To *Ski Centre*	*Rocky trails from summit back to Lochan buidhe – head west of cairn Lochan, follow gentle slope leading to ski centre.*	*4.7m*	*1.5 hours*
To			
To			
		Total Time	*11.2 hours*

Escape routes			
From *Ford of Avon, 042032*			
To *Glenmore lodge*	*From ford travel north/east follow track off slopes of Bynack More via coire odhar (048076) to lochan uaine (green loch) 001105)*	*8.3 miles*	*2.5 hours*
From			
To			
Naismith Rule – always allow for slowest person. And whoever is carrying the most gear.	Add 10 minutes per hour for rests	*1 hour, 50 minutes*
• One hour for every 3 miles or 5 kms. • One hour for every 2000 feet or 600m gained	Total estimate time for trip	*13 hours*

Figure 8 – Example route card

Bike and Foot Grades

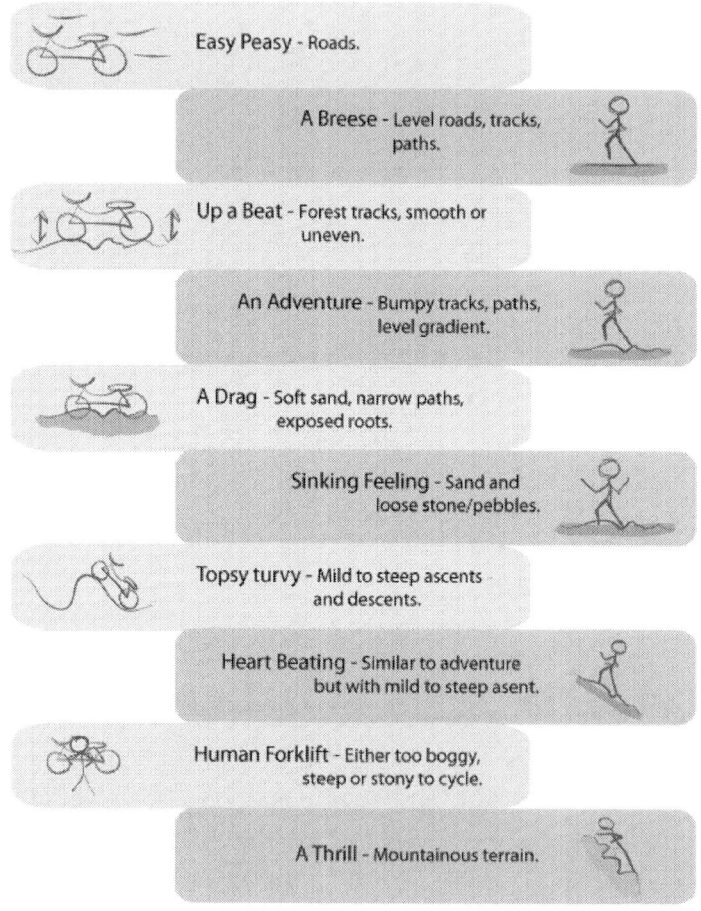

Figure 9 – Grades of both routes based on a 40 year old of mid range fitness.

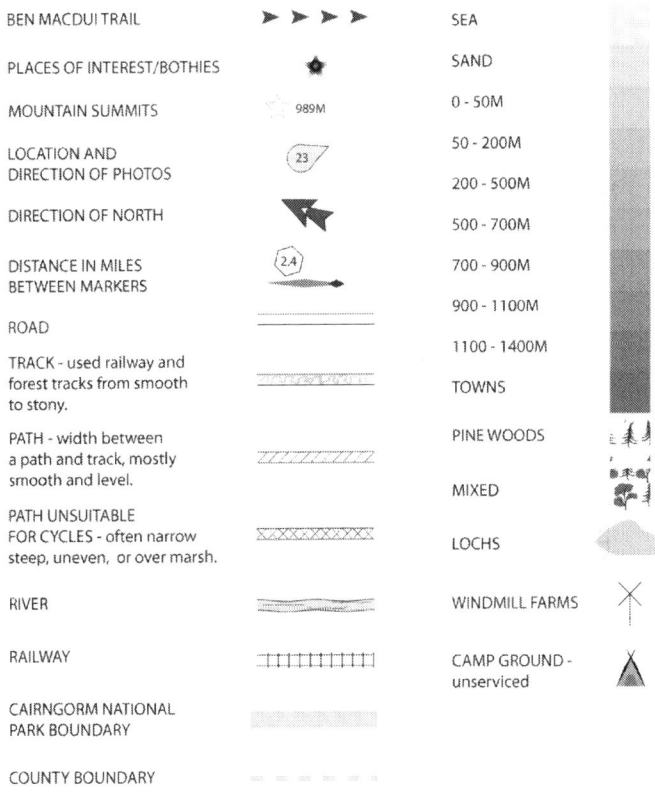

BEN MACDUI TRAIL		SEA
PLACES OF INTEREST/BOTHIES		SAND
MOUNTAIN SUMMITS	989M	0 - 50M
LOCATION AND DIRECTION OF PHOTOS	23	50 - 200M
		200 - 500M
DIRECTION OF NORTH		500 - 700M
DISTANCE IN MILES BETWEEN MARKERS	2.4	700 - 900M
		900 - 1100M
ROAD		1100 - 1400M
TRACK - used railway and forest tracks from smooth to stony.		TOWNS
PATH - width between a path and track, mostly smooth and level.		PINE WOODS
PATH UNSUITABLE FOR CYCLES - often narrow steep, uneven, or over marsh.		MIXED
		LOCHS
RIVER		WINDMILL FARMS
RAILWAY		CAMP GROUND - unserviced
CAIRNGORM NATIONAL PARK BOUNDARY		
COUNTY BOUNDARY		

SCALE ON EACH MAP VARIES - PLEASE USE MILAGE MARKERS AS AN INDICATION OF DISTANCE.

PARTS OF ROUTE WHICH HAVE NO DISTINCT PATH OR TRACK SUCH AS ON THE CAIRNGORMS AND MARSH AREAS ARE LEFT BLANK.

Figure 10 - Map Legend for the Ben Macdui Trail maps

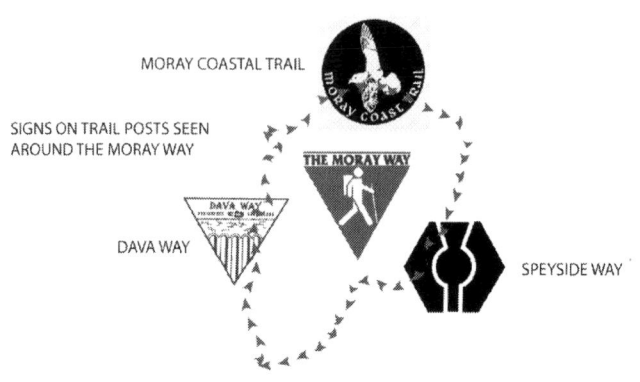

MORAY COASTAL TRAIL

SIGNS ON TRAIL POSTS SEEN
AROUND THE MORAY WAY

THE MORAY WAY

DAVA WAY

SPEYSIDE WAY

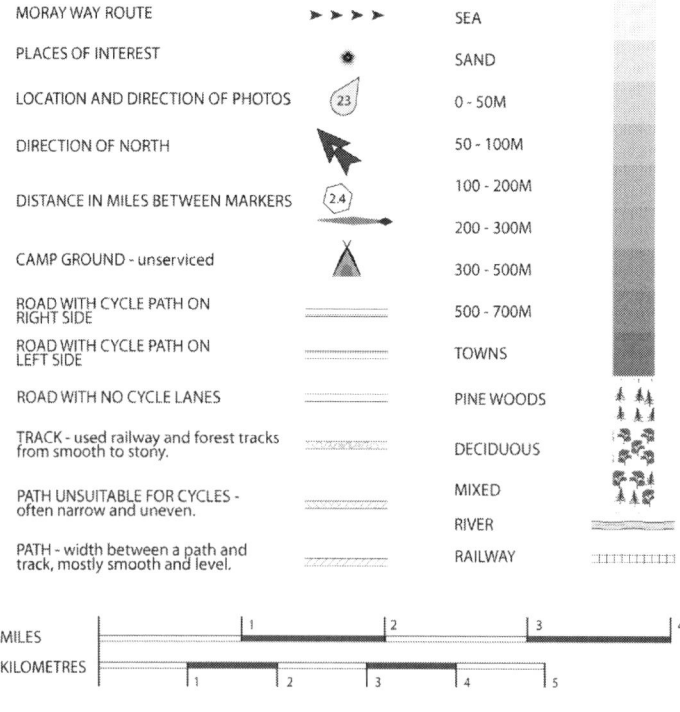

MORAY WAY ROUTE	➤➤➤➤	SEA
PLACES OF INTEREST		SAND
LOCATION AND DIRECTION OF PHOTOS	23	0 - 50M
DIRECTION OF NORTH		50 - 100M
DISTANCE IN MILES BETWEEN MARKERS	24	100 - 200M
		200 - 300M
CAMP GROUND - unserviced		300 - 500M
ROAD WITH CYCLE PATH ON RIGHT SIDE		500 - 700M
ROAD WITH CYCLE PATH ON LEFT SIDE		TOWNS
ROAD WITH NO CYCLE LANES		PINE WOODS
TRACK - used railway and forest tracks from smooth to stony.		DECIDUOUS
PATH UNSUITABLE FOR CYCLES - often narrow and uneven.		MIXED
		RIVER
PATH - width between a path and track, mostly smooth and level.		RAILWAY

MILES
KILOMETRES

Figure 11 – Map legend for the Moray Way Maps

36

THE MORAY WAY – An introduction

The Moray Way was created a few years ago from the amalgamation of three existing walks, these being The Dava Way, The Moray Coastal Trail and The Speyside Way.

Length – 96 miles (155 km)

Total Ascent – 2,016m (6,614ft)

Highest point – 330m (1,083ft)

It is over 90 miles long and shaped like a triangle......sounds quite normal when just its facts and figures are listed but for a comparatively compact circular route, it is in fact very unique.

Aside from being a circular route, meaning the start and exit are at the same place and could very well be anywhere along it. Each of its three sides involves going over completely different terrain from one another.

If you love the sand, the gentle rolling of the waves, clear sea water to swim in, pine forests, spotting multitudes of sea birds and exploring hidden caves, then you'll love the Coastal part of the route from Findhorn to Kingston.

Next is the route down the River Spey from its ever-changing mouth where its torrent endlessly shifts the sands as well as sometimes bridges in bad spates. It is the main artery out of Moray for runoff from the high Cairngorms and surrounding hills, and some might say the main reason of Morays fame for its many Whiskies (which you start smelling past Craigellachie) and salmon fishing. From Kingston to Grantown on Spey you get the chance to see the hidden sides to this most majestic of rivers from its banks and above in the pine clad hills along its length.

The final stretch takes you far from the populated areas you have seen thus far out of the historic home base of the clan Grant over a fairly even and gentle climb up to the moors. Following in the rail tracks which really opened up the wonders of moray to the masses seeking the same peace, isolation and clean air you can still experience.

Have a safe journey.

THE MORAY WAY – The Basics

Stage 1 - **Forres to Findhorn** – OS sheet 27, 28, 423

Distance – 4.8 miles   Height gain/loss – 0m/18m

By bike -   By foot -

Route – Cycle path most of the way until the entrance to Findhorn foundation at NJ050635. Path changes side of road at NJ062611. At traffic lights NJ064616 carry on taking first right to see Kinloss cathedral or turn left to Findhorn. After foundation, follow road to marina.

Alternative routes/short cuts – Take right hand turning at NJ045637 for Heath House and follow to beach car park.

Findhorn to Burghead

Distance – 6.9 miles   Height gain/loss – 14m/0m

By bike -   By foot -

Route – When the tide is out sand is firm enough to ride on by tidemark, exit by Caravan Park in Burghead, turn left and follow road to Pict fort. When tide is in use soft sand/pebble track past dunes and RAF Kinloss, ground firms up from here and leads into forest where vehicle tracks lead past car park then to old railway line – follow to road, turn left to Pict fort.

Alternative routes/short cuts – After railway track go straight over Grant Street and follow road to right side of large building to join up with coastal path.

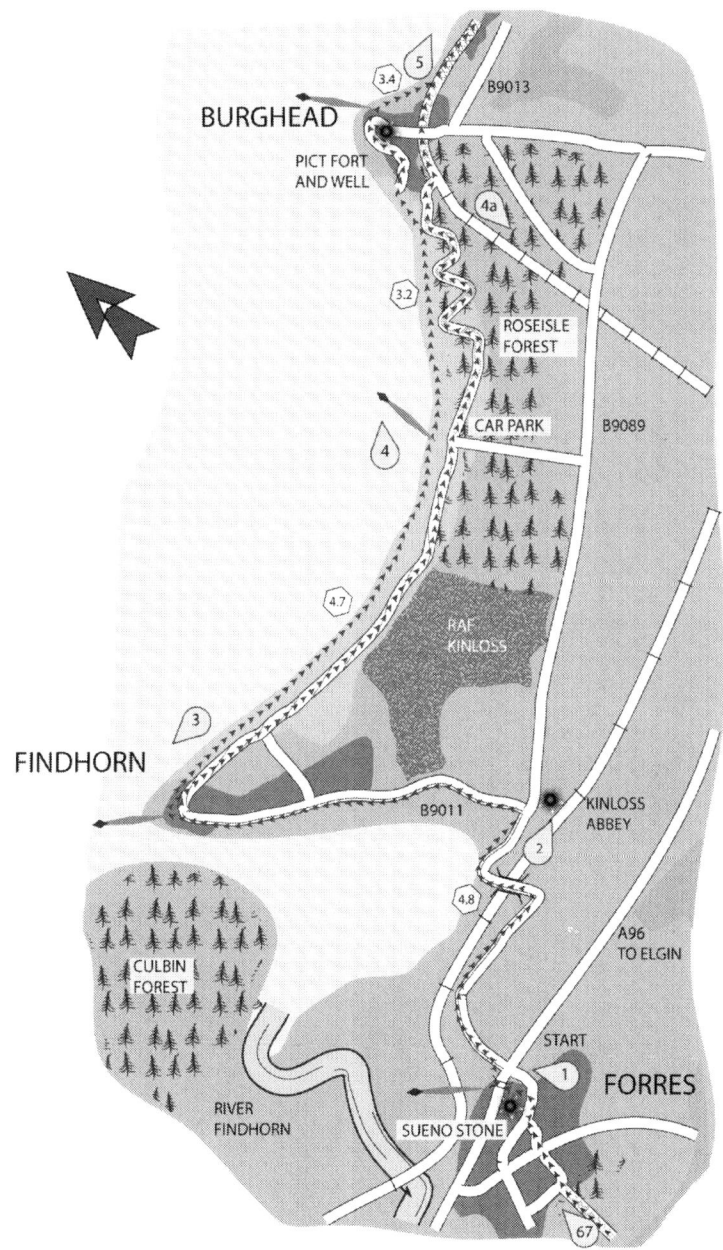

Stage 1 – Forres to Burghead

Stage 2 - **Burghead to Clashach Cove** – OS sheet 28, 423, 424

Distance – 3.4 miles   Height gain/loss – 37m/0m

By bike -   By foot -

Route – From fort follow coast line onto level track to Hopeman, ascend bank to path leading to road, follow along coast leading to firm path to Clashach Cove, path starts narrow progressing to wider with lots of ups and downs. May have to carry bike on approach to Clashach Cove.

Alternative routes/short cuts – For cycling, follow road out of Burghead, and turn left onto B9040 for Lossiemouth.

Clashach Cove to WW 2 Coastal Defences

Distance – 9.1 miles   Height gain/loss – 0m/48m

By bike -   By foot -

Route – Path starts wide, progressing to narrow, bumpy and near cliff edges after lookout tower to Covesea. Descends to beach of soft sand, follow round past lighthouse to Lossiemouth leading to grass slope and road. Follow coastal road round to Foot Bridge. Soft sand to WW2 Coastal Defences

Alternative routes/short cuts – For cycling stay on road to Lossiemouth, follow coastal road and just before footbridge veer off right on level track to B9103. Take first left after bridge over River Lossie onto track; go straight ahead from car park, first right and left at T-junction to defences.

For walking, when tide is in leave path at Covesea to B9040 or lighthouse (NJ204713) to road. **Remember** – you will get trapped if exploring the sculpture cave while tide is coming in.

Wild Camping at WW2 Coastal Defences, no water or toilets available.

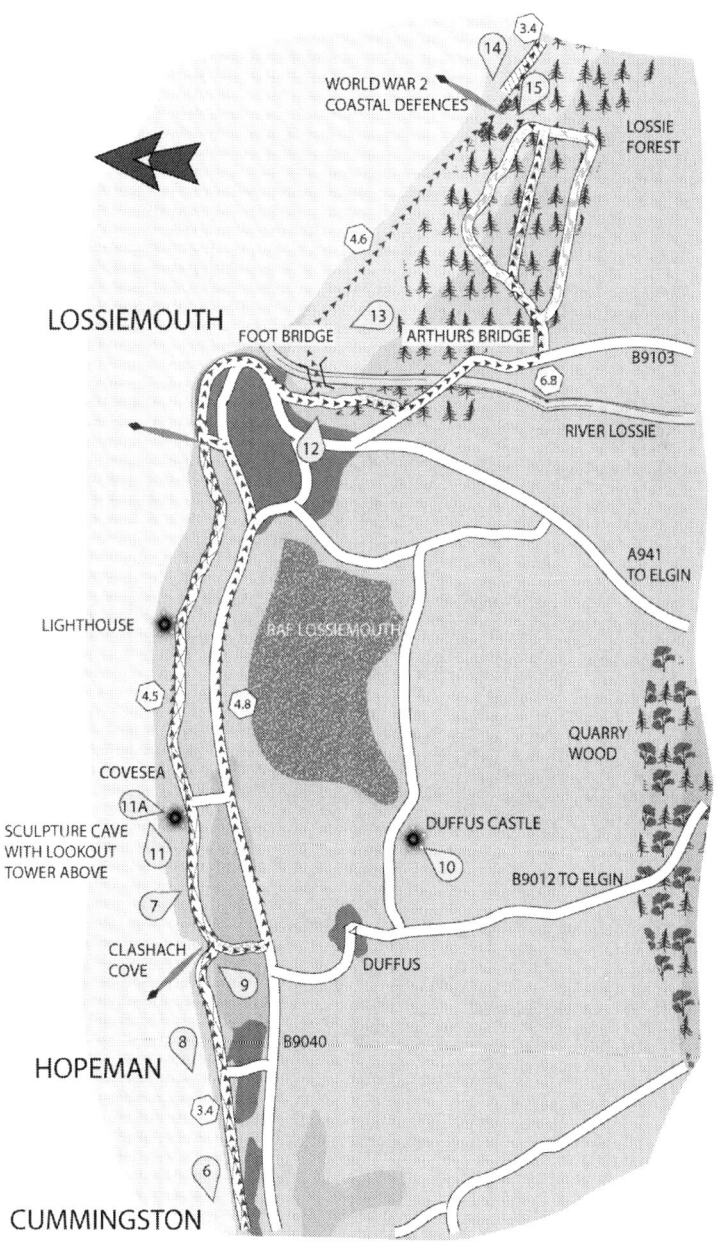

Stage 2 – Burghead to WW2 Coastal Defences

Stage 3 – **WW 2 Coastal Defences to Kingston** – OS sheet 28, 424

Distance – 3.4 miles   Height gain/loss – 16m/0m

By bike -

By foot -

Route – Sand and pebble rough level path leading to firm vehicle track from firing range to road at start of Kingston.

Kingston to Fochabers

Distance – 5 miles   Height gain/loss – 14m/0m

By bike -

By foot -

Route – Upon entering Kingston, take narrow path first right between houses leading to view point path to Garmouth. Follow road through town past shop take first left, then track on left down to level firm track across viaduct, turn first right and follow rough firm vehicle track until deviation turn left along narrow path leading to vehicle track. Turn right towards river then left onto firm bumpy path through woodland, follow under road and Rail Bridge over River Spey. Follow wide path along river past people of Fochabers monument to stony wide path leading up into Fochabers, follow to second bridge over river, turn right, go along right of school to roundabout take track between house and school, turn left along rough track to road, turn right follow up out of Fochabers.

Alternative routes/short cuts – For Cyclists avoid climb to view point at Kingston by following road to Garmouth. Avoid the few narrow paths by following path across viaduct to B9104.

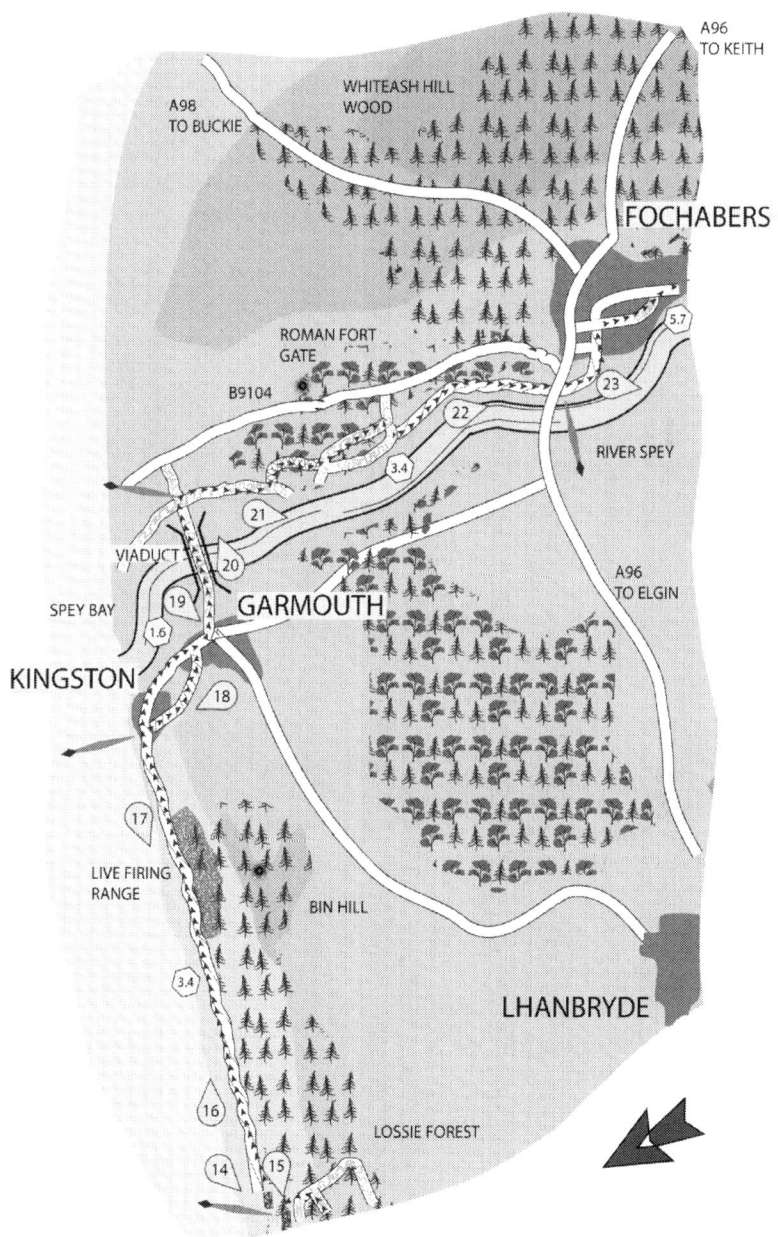

Stage 3 – WW 2 Coastal Defences to Fochabers

Stage 4 – **Fochabers to Boat O'Brig** – OS sheet 28, 424

Distance – 3.4 miles   Height gain/loss – 119m/100m

By bike -   By foot -

Route – Follow road to bridge under railway at Boat O'Brig, this stretch contains a lot of ups and downs from steep to gradual climbs and drops. Going in this direction the climbs are mostly gradual apart from in the middle where the road dips sharply over a river.

Boat O'Brig to Craigellachie

Distance – 9.1 miles   Height gain/loss – 250m/224m

By bike -   By foot -

Route – Follow road to traffic lights and take narrow steep path just before Road Bridge over the River Spey. Follow signs as path progresses to a rough track climbing up past farmhouse onto smooth track, follow to forest entrance on right, veer to right taking rough track along edge of forest leading up to gravel firm track, which involves two stages of going up and down steeply ending with long gradual drop to road leading to Craigellachie. At junction, turn right over bridge next to white pub (Fiddichside Inn) follow road take first left leads to camping spot and toilets.

Free camping, water and toilets offered here.

Alternative routes/short cuts – To Avoid narrow steep path, turn left under bridge up road to smooth vehicle track on right leading to forest entrance., but beware this road is narrow in places and used by distillery artics.

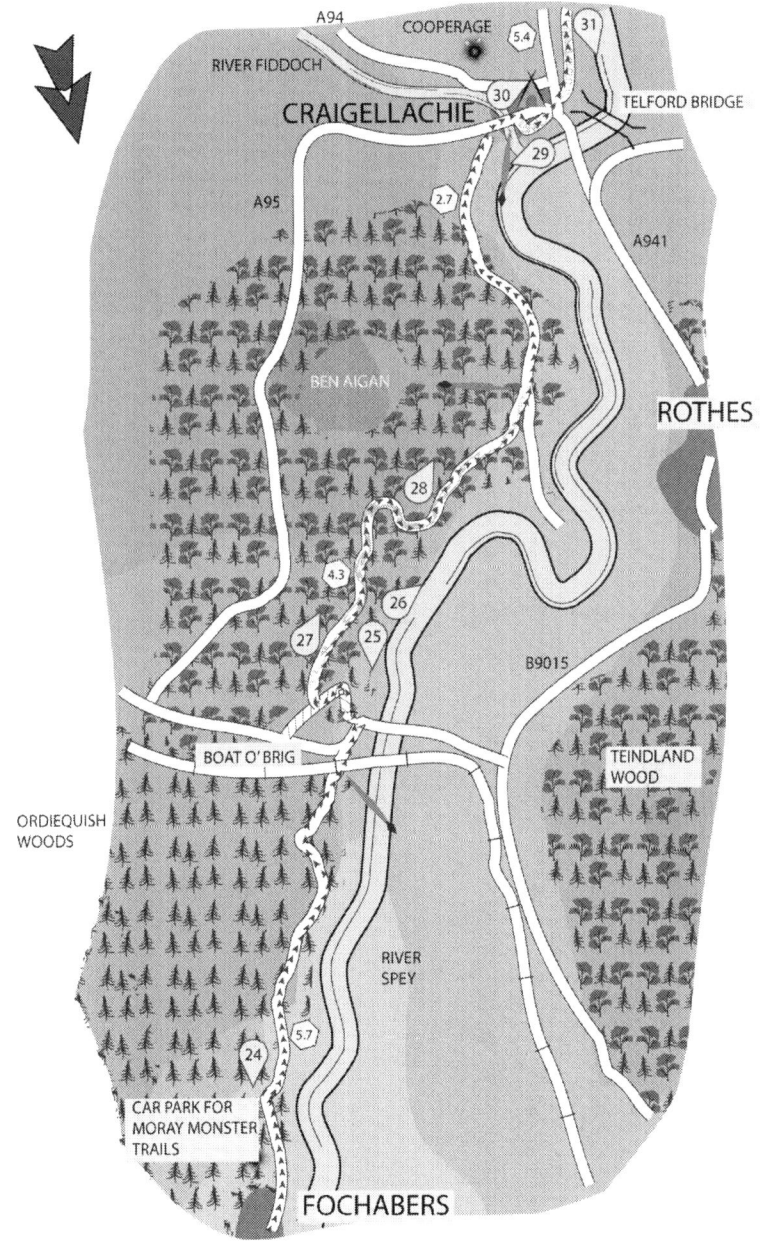

Stage 4 - Fochabers to Craigellachie

Stage 5 – **Craigellachie to Carron** – OS sheet 28, 424, 419

Distance – 6 miles   Height gain/loss – 34m/0m

By bike -   By foot -

Route – From Camping spot follow level wide track under bridge round past play ground up under the road bridge turn right to a tunnel under A95 and follow towards Aberlour. Within Aberlour follow path leading left of playground, leads to narrow wooden bridge back onto wide firm track, and involves a gentle climb leading to road into Carron just before bridge crossing. Follow road over bridge, turn left at junction then right just before distillery.

Carron to Cragganmore

Distance – 5.1 miles   Height gain/loss – 32m/0m

By bike -   By foot -

Route – Upon turning right onto track this leads directly to Cragganmore, any climbing is gradual and track is mainly firm but can get over grown and wet. Contains a lot of farm gates but you do not need to dismount to gain access round them. Several wooden bridges and one other narrow one are crossed before coming to the larger bridge across the River Spey into Cragganmore. Follow track passed disused station building.

Toilets and free camping offered at Cragganmore and at Blackboat.

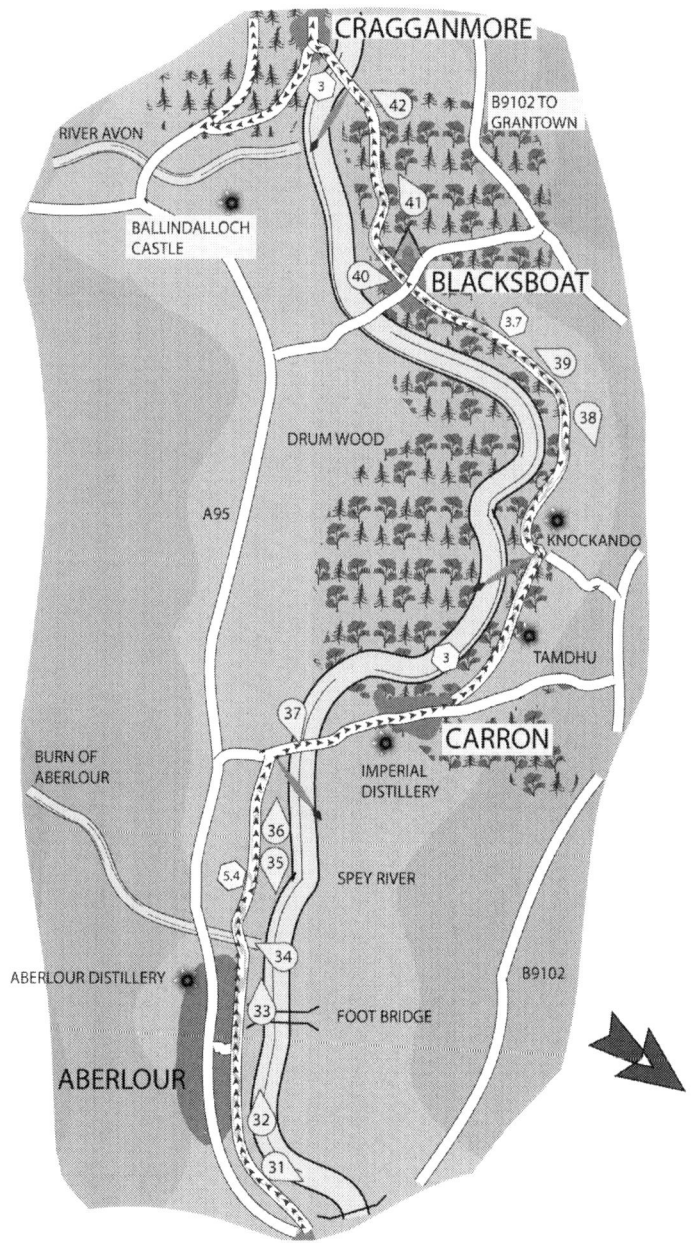

Stage 5 - Craigellachie to Cragganmore

Stage 6 – **Cragganmore to Mains of Dalvey,** OS sheet 28, 36, 419, 418

Distance – 4.3 miles   Height gain/loss – 199m/162m

By bike -   By foot -

Route – follow track along river then turn left and follow steep rough path through fields until gaining access to A95, follow rough path on left side of road, then turn left up through trees to forest and forest track. Path twists and turns from here via fields and forest tracks with many of the guillotine gates (photo 45) as access between them, eventually leading onto a B road above Mains of Dalvey. The route is well marked.

Alternative routes/short cuts – For Cyclists it's better to take road from Cragganmore up to A95 and follow to Mains of Dalvey.

Mains of Dalvey to Grantown on Spey

Distance – 7.5 miles   Height gain/loss – 96m/62m

By bike -   By foot -

Route – Cross road and gain access onto narrow path leading to forest track, follow track round until desent to A95, cross road turn right to track leading down towards River Spey and level straight firm wide track on left. Follow past Cromdale old station, under road bridge turn left leading to road past church across River Spey taking track on left down and around onto farm track leading to well maintained forest track to Grantown on Spey. At road junction from forest track turn right then immediate left follow road over Grantown High Street straight up past the Coop store to campsite and continuation of route.

Alternative routes/short cuts – For Cyclists either turn left on this quiet B road and follow up and around to Cromdale or right down to Mains of Dalvey and use the busy A95.

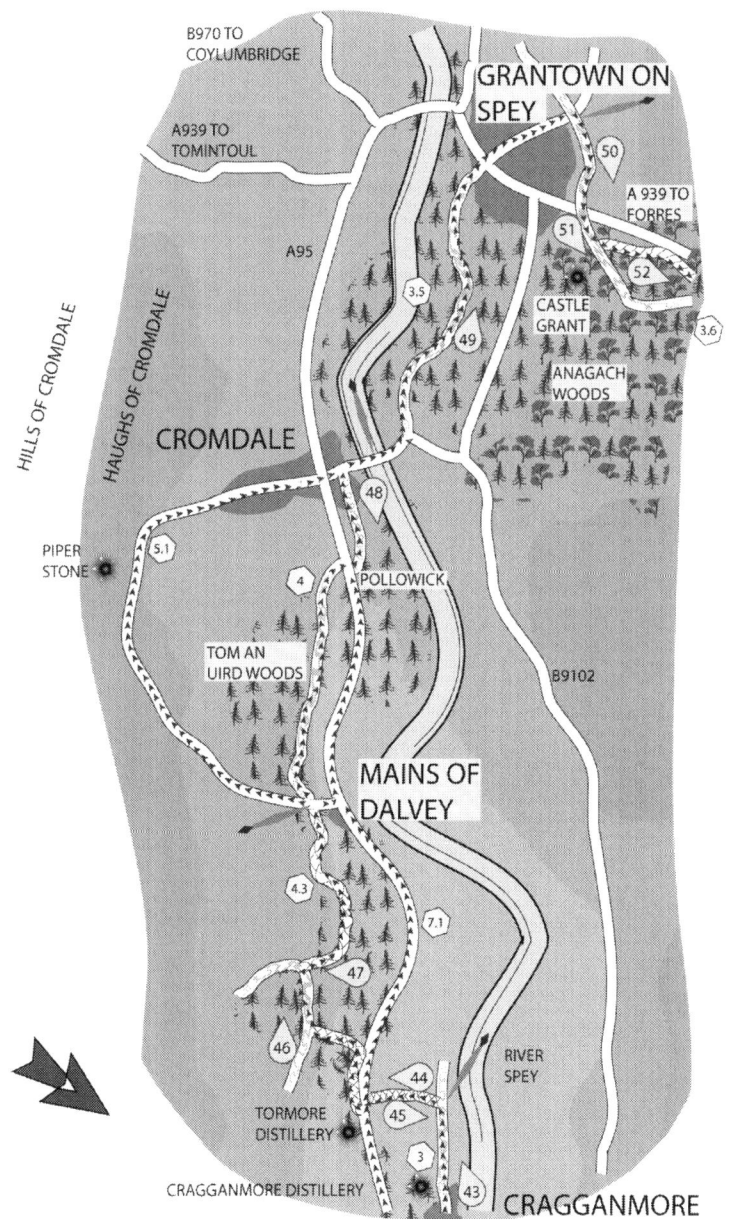

Stage 6 - Cragganmore to Grantown on Spey

Stage 7 – **Grantown on Spey to Dava** – OS sheet 36, 27, 419, 418

Distance – 8.4 miles   Height gain/loss – 106m/30m

By bike -   By foot -

Route – Use track past Campsite to under bridge then immediate right up firm path to level wide track. Gradual climb leads to the A939, then turn left onto narrow rough track running alongside A939 then turn down road to Lynmore taking track on left before house through woodland leading back to level firm track. Follow out onto moor land involving gentle climb to summit, then gradual descent to Dava. Follow detour round private property through woods on narrow path back onto track. Parts of track near to summit can be extremely boggy and wet.

Alternative routes/short cuts – For Cyclists to avoid narrow path upon Dava detour follow track to A940, cycle on road to steep track on right side past collection of sheds and buildings. This road can be busy.

Dava to Divie Viaduct

Distance – 4.7 miles   Height gain/loss – 0m/100m

By bike -   By foot -

Route – Track leads directly to Divie viaduct but involves some farm gates which do need to be opened and closed and involves going over some exposed areas with few trees to offer shelter. Track can be rough in places involving boggy areas and rough large stones.

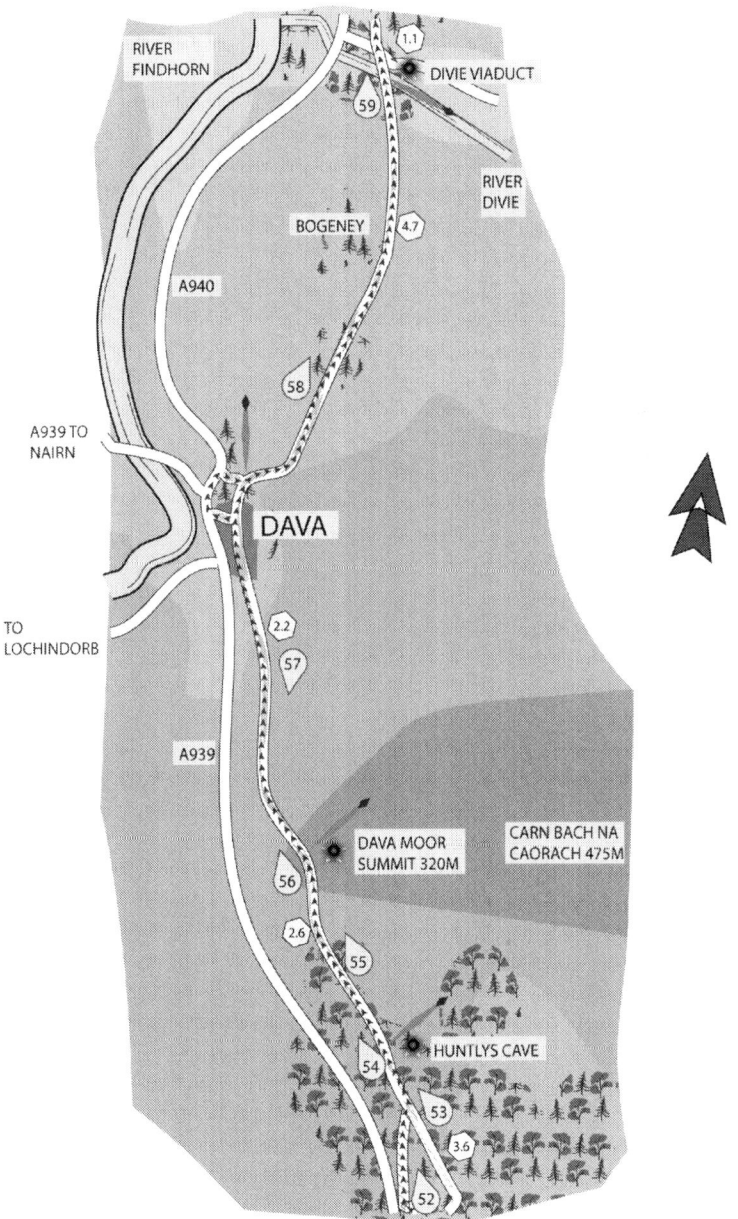

RIVER
FINDHORN

1.1

DIVIE VIADUCT

59

RIVER
DIVIE

BOGENEY

4.7

A940

58

A939 TO
NAIRN

DAVA

TO
LOCHINDORB

2.2

57

A939

DAVA MOOR
SUMMIT 320M

CARN BACH NA
CAORACH 475M

56

2.6

55

HUNTLYS CAVE

54

53

3.6

52

Stage 7 - Grantown on Spey to Divie Viaduct

Stage 8 - **Divie Viaduct to Forres** – OS sheet 27, 419, 423

Distance – 10.5 miles   Height gain/loss – 0m/169m

By bike -    By foot -

Route – Track carries on and rough in places leading to a rough narrow path detouring boggier parts of the track, rejoining it by the breathing space at Dunphail. Carry on track under bridge through farm land which despite being firm crosses lots of farm gates in the next 3.5 miles. Across road by Clashdhu follow track which narrows over two bridges, under one bridge and up onto another leading to a deviation up through the woods via a rough boggy path with exposed roots rejoining the level track at Woodside. Follow this to a housing estate road in Forres, turn right follow to top where there is a small gap between houses (easy to miss) which allows access to another estate road leading down past lake, then the school. At junction turn right, straight over round about follow round past large park on right, at junction turn right which leads back to Sueno stone and end. Well done.

If you'd like to know more detail about some parts of this route, then please refer to 'The detail' and its corresponding chapters to each stage where types of woodlands, plants and particular difficult path sections are discussed.

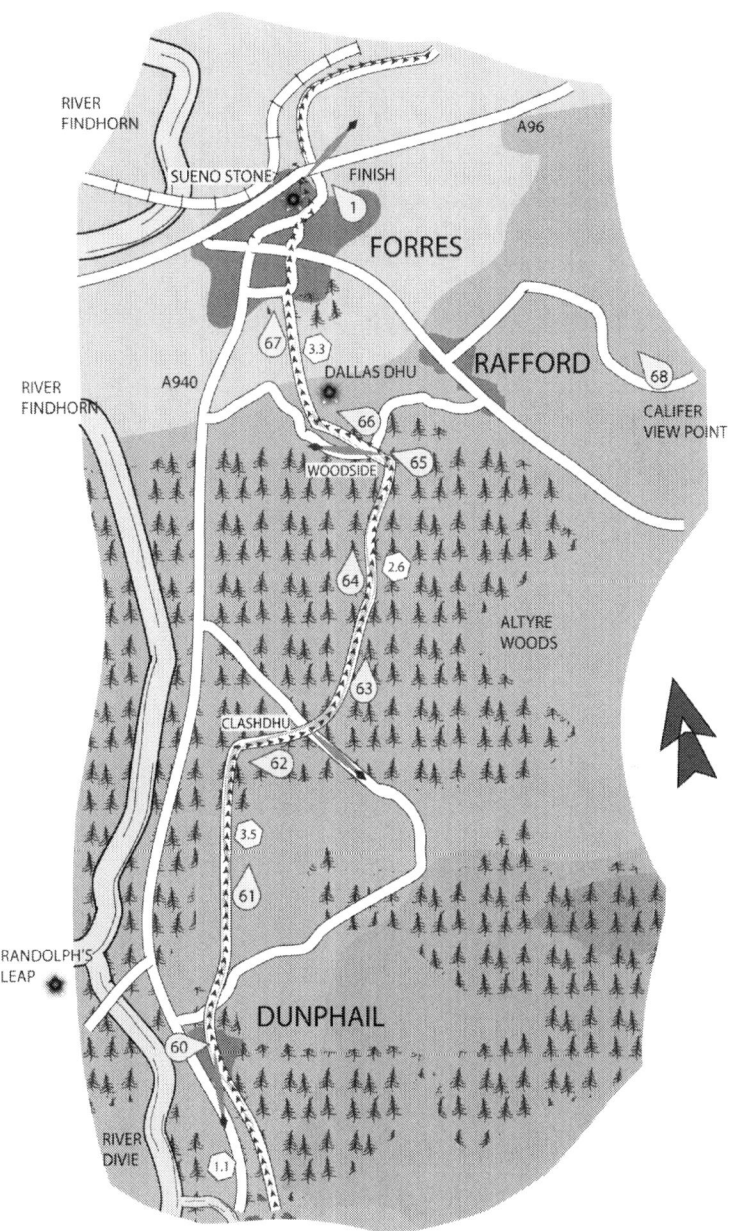

RIVER
FINDHORN

A96

SUENO STONE

FINISH

1

FORRES

67

3.3

DALLAS DHU

RAFFORD

68

RIVER
FINDHORN

A940

CALIFER
VIEW POINT

66

WOODSIDE

65

64

2.6

ALTYRE
WOODS

63

CLASHDHU

62

3.5

61

RANDOLPH'S
LEAP

DUNPHAIL

60

RIVER
DIVIE

1.1

Stage 8 - Divie Viaduct to Forres

THE MORAY WAY – The Detail

Stage 1 - **Forres to Findhorn** – OS sheet 27, 28, 423

Distance – 4.8 miles   Height gain/loss – 0m/18m

The night had been savage under the dark steamy clouds. When dawn broke, what was left of them faded away under the hot morning sun creating a fine low mist as all ground water was boiled and evaporated.

The carts wheels cracked and groaned under immense weight as it progressed unseen along the narrow track, while the feeble collection of people waited in fear and mourning for their lost ones.

Suddenly a shout was heard followed by impenetrable silence when only the sharp breathing of the tired and weary beast dragging the wagon could be heard copying the thumping of hearts of all present in anticipation of its arrival. Orders were shouted and the running of feet exploded amidst this silence as the great stone years in the making was slowly raised into place by rope, wood, sweat and pulsing muscles……..

Over 1,000 years later and that stone, known as the Sueno Stone standing 6m high covered on all sides from top to bottom with symbols and drawings of old is still standing for all to see in near perfect condition despite a millennium of strong westerly winds, the rain and bloody human history. Making it as good a place as any to start this route in a direction, which would ensure that those strong winds aid you along the exposed coastal part and not beat you back.

Most important thing to remember at this point is do not just rush off over the spanking new white footbridge and on along the cycle path to Kinloss. Rather take some time to look around the four varied faces of the Sueno stone. Of intricate Celtic curves and interweaving lines, recoding a battle where enemies met and charged with lance, sword and shield under the screams of death and malice. The record of victory is particularly poignant seeing the fate of the loser's heads. In addition, the extent and detail of the carvings only reflects more than any supposition of the presence of supreme and skilled artisans amidst these savage times.

If only it could talk, not only would it have many true stories to tell of the events and conflicts around Forres but perhaps it could solve the greatest mystery of all, that being the reason for its existence.

Many believe that Sueno stone was made by the church as a reminder to the constant conflicts in this region, of good over evil. While many more still hold onto the belief that only the feelings left upon the aftermath of fierce battles would give reason for such a costly and meaningful statue to man's loss to be made.

Around 844AD, Moray was an independent region led by leaders called the Maormars who migrating from Argyll to escape the invading Scandinavians only to have them invade their new home. Maelbrigd or more commonly known as 'Tooth' unwilling to run again set forth to challenge 'Sigurd the powerful' the Norseman's leader. Unfortunately, the tactful deceiving of Sigurd won the day and they marched from the battlefield with the losers heads bobbing around their gear. (The head chopping giving it an association with the stone)

Maelbrigd was named 'tooth' due to a large tooth protruding from his mouth, which in death allowed him to wreak his revenge upon Sigurd who had his head. This tooth scrapes Sigurd skin, infesting him with a gangrenous infection (no such thing as Colgate back then!) killing him three days later. The location of the stone is said to mark his grave.

Fast forward now to 1000AD and the Danes, under a leader called 'Sueno' (the matching names giving raise to its association with the stone) came to the shores of Moray to spill blood and other numerous naughty things, they were met by the combined forces of the Scots under Malcolm ll, king of Scotland. Suffice to say is that the Scots lost to an army of veterans.

However, not to be out done, Malcolm gathered another better army 60 years later and in the face of defeat spurned his men onto final victory by charging sword raised into the thick of the unorganized enemy. The association to this 'Battle of Mortlach' to the stone is said to be within the treaty drawn up after between Malcolm and his enemies. Creating a period of peace, that was seen as a far greater reason to celebrate, with

Photo 1 – Sueno Stone

Photo 2 – Kinloss Abbey

the men back from their manly games and able once more to fertilize field and lassies.

As you make your way along the nice level road to Kinloss, it is hard to imagine that once this whole area was covered in dense woodland. Much harder to travel through and easier to get lost in; bring us nicely to the creation of Kinloss abbey. While it existed, before reformation caused many seats of religion to relinquish their huge assets of land and money, it provided an important place of learning for local nobles and resting place for royalty and soldiers alike. Amongst its gardens of wondrous herbs, a library full of vast knowledge and a kitchen where cooks used the fruits from their land, as well as a chapel for prayer.

But before all that during a hunting party around 1150AD, the leader, David 1, king of Scotland got separated from the party and was only rescued by the attentions of a white dove leading him to a clearing. It was late in the day and he was thankful for the shelter offered by a Shepard for the night during which he dreamt of the Virgin Mary, who asked in return for saving him to build a sacred building within the clearing. Upon returning to Duffus castle where he was staying he quickly organized for the best architects to start building straight away, and the rest as they say is history!

Upon entering Kinloss passing through the traffic lights and taking the right hand track, the ruin that this leads to does not suitably reflect the abbeys size and importance to the locality but the tombstones certainly make for some interesting reading.

Nowadays the local's concerns centre around the RAF camp, whose quarters you see around you and long runway on the road leading to village of Findhorn. For over 70 years, this camp (along with RAF Lossiemouth) has been a base from which the air forces of the UK have provided security around the world, but (unlike RAF Lossiemouth) this camps days are numbered.

Scheduled to be closed by 2015 it is worth a look down the runway as you pass it on the right and perhaps get a glimpse of the fleet of Nimrods (if still there). No more will they fill the skies with their poetic flight, their grace and ease of movement like that of a swan, very different to the roar of the super jets at RAF Lossiemouth.

Photo 3 – Looking towards Findhorn

Photo 4 – Looking towards Burghead

On the left side of the road just past the runway is a hide from which it is possible to see the flight of birds, who love the marshy and coastal estuary of the River Findhorn. Huge in breadth and width, a good pair of binoculars and good zoom lens could provide some memorable sights.

Just up the road abit more is the World-renowned Findhorn Foundation, which you either know a lot about or have never heard of before. Whichever, their enlightened approach to life is worth exploring, as well as their bread. The skills portrayed in the pottery shop are only equaled by the eco art displayed in the Moray Art Centre but perhaps nowhere as good as the paintings on the Foundations Four wind turbines which can be seen upon crossing the sand dunes towards Burghead.

You now enter Findhorn village after the turning for the foundation and have to walk on the pavement or cycle on the road leading past the roundhouse on the left then through pine woodland. Just past this is the right hand turning towards the sand dunes car park and detour round Findhorn, but why rush when there is so much more to see and enjoy, especially the soft vanilla ice cream from the marina café, which you could enjoy while sitting at the captain's table!

On the long straight down towards the marina, the views on offer on the left are of the estuary and the many small and large boat landings, plus on the far bank can be seen the start of the immense Culbin forest stretching from here all the way to Nairn.

If you were standing here in the 17th century, you would have seen what was called the 'Granary of Moray' of fields and small settlements instead of trees. Going by finds of early man's tools the area was used since we first arrived here, on and off in-between the local battles between land and sea. Fast forward to the early 18th century and an immense stretch of sand dunes would present itself to you covering all dwellings and fields.

The reason was the fierce winds and storms, which will always move about the coastal sands of Moray, and specifically on one unforgettable night in the late 17th century. After seven centuries of relative, calm a night of wild winds, enveloped the area forever in tones of sand. Was it Mother Nature just organizing her pantry? Or as legend has it, was it the cruel blasphemous lairds fault for playing cards one Saturday night into the Sabbath shouting upon being told this that he would play all day if he wanted to, with the devil as his partner!!!

Apart from now thinking 'bad, bad laird' you may be wondering how a desert of sand was converted into woodland supporting numerous wild animals such as the elusive red squirrel and badger plus hundreds of different species of flora. It was not easy, first Marram Grass was tried but failed at stabilizing the sand, and then the never-ending task of thatching the sand with brushwood was tried and succeeded. Upon this stable ground, numerous species of pine were tried with Corsican Pine being the most successful. If you have time, you can see the small areas in culbin where these different types were tested from the Welhill Car Park, just take the left hand path as you enter the Car Park and follow it as it twists and turns for about 1 mile.

Back to Findhorn, you are probably passing the first of two pubs and on a hot day is the last place before Burghead to wet you whiskers. Follow the road round to the right and take the left turning towards the marina, or alternatively take the path hugging the River Findhorn opposite the Kimberley Inn leading you to the marina café and a great viewpoint of the busy little port.

After the soft vanilla ice cream treat head west to the sand dunes leading to Burghead or if the tide is out you cannot really leave this town without seeing its resident herd of seals. If you do then just follow the estuary as it curves round towards the culbin looking back at Findhorn harbour just before going over the dunes, at sunset the colours can be quite fantastic off the boats, buildings and calm water.

On the other side of the dunes, you should see the black mass of the seals at the end of the exposed sand bank or even on the Culbin side if too many people are present. The stretch of River Findhorn along these dunes is very deep and tidal so swimming is not advised away from the protected cove just past the marina.

Findhorn as a working fishing and shipping port has been around for a long time, the town you see today is the third with the others being swept away or flooded by the same storms, which desolated culbin. The first Findhorn was said to of stood well out into the Moray Firth meaning it could well of been far beyond where you see the seals, the second is recorded to have been a mile north west of the present town meaning that the seals are laying around on top of it.

This second town was to all accounts, thriving with warehouses, shipping produce all over the continent but the ever-shifting sands made its port shallower and stated to encroach onto the houses of the sailors and fisherman. Eventually the present town was planned and built, until like the culbin in the space of one night all the buildings and what was Findhorn the 2nd disappeared under the surf and sand.

Findhorn to Burghead

Distance – 6.9 miles   Height gain/loss – 14m/0m

Now it may seem strange why a town was built so far out into the firth on sand in the first place, once when the culbin was fertile the bay between Findhorn and Burghead did not curve as it does today. Rather it was similar to that between Lossiemouth and Garmouth with a distance of only 5 miles between the towns instead of the seven today. Not to mean that it would have been easier to get between the two as this moorland was covered in high dunes and exposed roots from the harvesting of tree's and the peat. All no doubt adding to the reasons why the coastline retreated in response to the sea.

The route so far has been on firm level ground, after the marina the going gets harder, if the tide is out the best bet is to walk or cycle near to the waves where the sand is firmer. In the event that the tide is in, the undefined track over pebbles and soft sand should be followed starting after the Car Park leading you past the Wind turbines of the Foundation then the high fences of the RAF camp.

If possible, the beach route can be very enjoyable, there are some pools of water that need negotiating but as you progress around the bay, the first of the many WW2 Coastal Defences come into view and apart from their historical significant provide ideal platforms to sunbath on.

Opportunities for sights of natural wonders are more likely while walking the sand dunes and through Roseisle forest but for sheer relaxation, inner peace and all that jazz, walking along the beach to the entry road into Burghead just cannot be beat.

If on the other hand, it is the natural wonders you would like to see or more than likely the tides in and a strong wind is blowing, the shelter of the pines is probably better. The only disadvantage of this is that the tracks in this forest, despite predominantly heading in a west/east

Photo 4a – Rail track leading to Burghead

Photo 5 – Disused rail track to Cummingston

direction do tend to twist and turn so apart from watching and admiring the many coastal plants on offer, also keep an eye on the map especially where tracks meet.

Before the Car Park, you will encounter markers of walks from there, the white being to a bird hide passing by feeders near the car park where red Squirrels can be seen. The track after the Car Park can get slightly confusing and you could as likely end up walking along the rail track rather than find the twisting track leading to Burghead. Walking along the rail track can be just as amusing; it is very unusual to see the tracks left in place and while walking along it with high banks either side the eerie silence can lead one to feel that you are going to hear the sounds of a steam train at any moment. Spooky!!

Stage 2 - **Burghead to Clashach Cove** – OS sheet 28, 423, 424

Distance – 3.4 miles   Height gain/loss – 37m/0m

Its 125AD, over 40 years since over 60,000 Picts met the legions under Agricola at the battle of Mons Graupius. Despite Agricola winning the day, the frontier of Moray proved difficult to totally subdue. As the Picts gained power, the Romans, in short supply of ore to fuel their Great War machine, needed deposits of ore found along the local coastline, and an unsteady truce developed between the two, the Romans gaining safe passage to these mines in exchange for coin. An early example of diplomacy at work.

It had been a long journey for the Trierarchus (ship commander) and his miles (sailors) aboard this Trireme (war ship) of the Classis Britannica fleet. Ahead of him was his final destination where, despite turning his stomach he was ordered to bow to the demands of this lands barbaric horde.

Before him lay the impenetrable fortress of Castra Alata (Burghead), of timber and turf ramparts guarding the rich and fertile lands surrounding the great loch of Spynie with the chieftain visible on the central ridge, large bearded and clothed in linen and hide. To his left the populace was making their way to its safety from a small gathering of wood and turf round huts with small Coracles resting outside them, over shadowed by the chieftain's residence on the hill of Clarkly.

The Romans or those that travelled over water, the 'Pict' in their sleek high bowed war ship with sail, wood and man all coated in green, were late. but amidst the camouflage the shining armour of the land devils was quite visible and the chieftain relaxed slightly and told his subordinates to cancel the alarm and made his way down through the ridges and ramparts to greet these new comers. For the wealth, they brought in gold and coin that would ensure his status and a day of joyous feasting ahead.

As technology advances and the archeologists dig deeper, the history we know is forever changing and the opening tale is one of many hypotheses' accounting for new finds such as the three large Roman coin hordes found in Moray, one on Clarkly hill above Burghead.

The fortress of Burghead is well known, first recorded by Aricote's Naval Fleet after the battle of Mons Graupius on a map drawn by Ptolemy. Although a type of defense has probably been there since the early settlers who would have seen this outcrop of rock as a place of safety to guard their winter food stock. They may have also started the Roman well as an obvious means of providing fresh water during a siege, later developed by those with the skills to do so. Although most towns had wells from which to gain fresh water before the invention of water pipes and taps.

When the Vikings arrived after the Romans had left, they easily swept aside any resistance the Moravians could conjure up and later improved the fortifications of Burghead using

Spynie Loch refers to a large tract of inland sea, which at that time covered the lowlands of Moray from Lossiemouth to Findhorn, over time it slowly drained helped later by man to provide the farmland you see today between this coastal stretch and Elgin and the A 96. The ruins of Spynie abbey were once where the harbour for Elgin was until Lossie replaced it, but more on that later. A Coracle is the small one-man boat the Picts used for fishing. The name Pict means 'painted people', which the picts could just as likely used as referenced to the camouflaged Roman sailors.

over 1000 local oak trunks. From that time on, Burghead saw its share of bitter battles and periods of peace and growth until the hardened Vikings left, leaving behind only those who wished to prosper within moray from the land and rich seas. They intermarried into the community and helped propel the local fishing trade into a mass market. Unfortunately, it was this important food source, which saw the final destruction of the 'winged camp' as the Romans called it when it was cleared away to build the harbour you can now see from the tip of Burghead on top of the

Photo 6 – Looking back to Burghead from Cummingston

Photo 7 – Possibilities of seeing sea Birds

white walled vantage point. The building of a new town of Burghead 100 years ago did not help much either.

From this vantage point you not only have great views over the firth, of where you've been and are going but on a certain day in July, you might see the Vikings of Glasgow. Along with the master storyteller Robert Low (Author of the Oathsworn Viking trilogy) as they act out battles of old, with the clash of steel, shields thundering together and the roar of hate during the 'Picnic with the Picts' event.

Before leaving the sights and sounds of the reinactors and following the rocky outcrops around the village to the disused railway line to Cummingston, it would be wise to recall some of this coastline historical jubilation. None more so than Burghead which as you know was the HQ of the Picts. An interesting race whose beginnings and end are both shrouded in the mist of uncertainty, myth and the dark blue face dye they developed from the Woad plant (at this time indigenous around the Mediterranean, and imported by picts from the Romans or tribes further south until they grew it).

First, it is generally excepted that they were already here being the ancestor of the early settlers with more connections to the people south of them rather than the growing Scots nation of Dál Riata on the west coast who they didn't even share the same language with being separated from them by the then impenetrable Highland mountains. As for their ending or disappearance, they did not, rather it was just a case of them blending together with other races that saw this land as a great place to emigrate to or invade.

Now for the myths started by medieval chroniclers to explain their lack of knowledge about them. Apparently, these Picts are in fact nomads from the steppes of Eastern Europe. They were Scythians, in fact just male Scythians (obviously no women fancied the trip) who sailed in small war ship finding their way through storms and high waves off the coast of Ireland. The Irish refused them entry but understanding the need for women, gave them some and they left to settle in a land they had obviously glimpsed but failed to land at. Apart from explaining a very unlikely place of their origin, it would however explain their method of kingship following the female line rather than the male.

Now onto their demise, this myth centers on what is called 'The treachery of Scone' set during times when a swordsmiths help was

Photo 8 – Looking back at Hopeman Harbour and Beach

Photo 9 – Clashach Cove

needed to get rid of unwanted people, where as today its lawyers! It was an old ploy but obviously new back then of when the royalty of the Picts were invited to a sumptuous meal by the royalty of the Scots. They were dined, wined, and made to feel right at home until from the same arch a group of nice dancers had just vacated the room from, there came warriors with raised swords and pop, off with the heads.

Onto more pleasant items, you should be approaching Cummingston now. Following the level track is the easiest way to do this but on a nice day taking a detour along the coastal rocky outcrops would serve to take you pass a few well known caves along this stretch. Some of the first offering shelter once to Jacobite soldiers from Hanoverian troops, and to local's up to the early 19th century. But be wary if you fear the Wyvers, or Spiders as there is probably plenty of them within.

Further, on you will find the high bouldering rocks just before the Town upon which you might see the experienced boulderers climbing pitches such as 'the dirty old man' or the 'kneewreaker chimney'. With all the sweating and climbers lingo flying around it is hard not to get caught up into the festivities of it all but perhaps worth staying awhile, if only to see if the small mattresses they use do actually break a fall!

If you decided to stay on the track, then your entry to the shores of Cummingston would have been through an arched bridge. This is a small town that like Hopeman further on was a planned village first called Port Cummings (despite not having one) built due to the demands of the growing fishing industry and was founded in 1808 consisting first of a row of stone built houses. Originally, it was meant to house fisherman but the lack of a harbour meant that only 30 years later farm labours and miners from local quarries mostly inhabited it. Its name comes from the Abbot Cumaine a follower of St. Columba who came from Ireland in mid 5th century to spread Christianity amongst the druid worshippers around Burghead.

Back on the track you are once more surrounded by embankments of broom and gorse in bloom; (June is best) fighting for the attentions of the flying fertilizers whose flowers similar in colour and appearance seem to cover the whole area in yellow, you might even see primrose. If you ventured along the rocky coast opportunities to view and photograph gulls, finches and shags abound while they rest on the coastal cliffs ledges.

Photo 10 - Duffus Castle

Eventually the nice level track ends just before a stone bridge. To the right of this are steps with a built-in channel on the left side to aid pushing a cycle over them rather than having to carry it. Follow the path over the bridge as it leads to the harbour road of Hopeman. From here, you can either follow the road round the harbour past the skate park onto a narrow path past beach huts and a golf course to Clashach Cove or turn right and cycle up to the B9040 and on to Lossiemouth.

Hopeman was created at the same time as Cummingston; when it was called Broad Hythe beforehand with a fishing station already insitu and a prominent headland enabling a harbour to be built giving it a better chance. Many Gaelic speaking families were brought to this new town, which had some teething problems involving the harbours condition but this was improved after 1818 when the Scots arrived on the scene chasing their prized herrings. It is interesting to note that like the green belt town of England, many different dialects survived in Moray at one point, meaning that a person could tell if you were from Elgin, Forres, or along the River Spey. These diminished as more people were brought in to new towns or moved here and after about the mid 18th century Gaelic was not spoken in schools any more. However, it is making a heck of a comeback now in places of learning throughout the highlands, especially the recently formed University of the Highlands and Islands. One other interesting item about these new towns and the merchant industry they supported is that most folk during these times had a nominal diet of cabbage. What must have it been like when a dad or son came home from far shores bringing with him strange and exotic produce?

There is a tale of a housewife who received a parcel of tea, news of which spread as fast around the small community. These days it would be laughable to wonder what you did with tea, but back then quite understandable and after preparing, it as she did her cabbage you can only wonder how good it tasted and just how long it took to find its true use!

Clashach Cove to WW 2 Coastal Defences

Distance – 9.1 miles   Height gain/loss – 0m/48m

Given the effort needed up the narrow eroded path from the golf course to Clashach cove, it is hard to imagine the grand sight that awaits you at the top. Its breath of width seems unbelievable, the kaleidoscope of colours (like multi coloured sherbet in a sweet jar) along its rock face only adds to realization that giants roamed these shore at one time, but the most awesome aspect is the two gapping black holes so small from where you are but huge down next to them.

The seaward cave is short in length, opening out onto the shore in the direction of Lossiemouth although access along this part of the shore is very dangerous due to the very likelihood of getting trapped by the tide. If the tide is out, you will be able to walk for some distance amongst the rubble of weather worn cliffs and stacks offering wondrous views and photographic opportunities of coastal birds, but keep an eye on the tide!

The larger and deeper of the two caves is the one of importance. As well as attracting many campers and over night revelers its use goes back far in time. A priest called Gernadius used it in the 10th century to spread the gospel in the most hospitable conditions he could find although the difference between a cave and a pre-central heated stone church could be negotiable. It is said also that a cave at Clashach Cove was used to

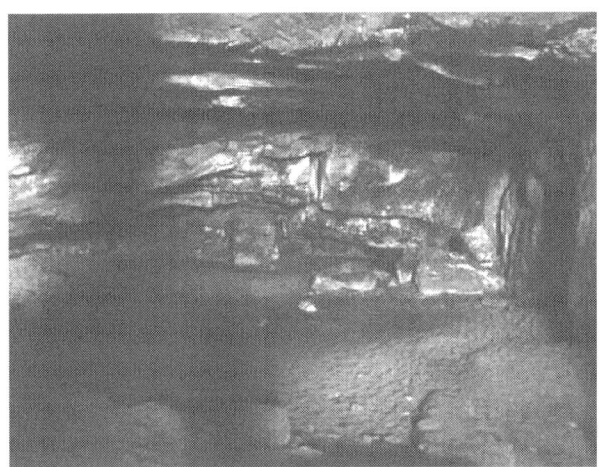

Photo 11A – Main chamber of Sculptors cave

Photo 11 – Sea stack seen from cliff edge path past lookout tower.

store the evil gains of smuggling, before being moved onto Gordonstoun via a tunnel within the cave. This tunnel has never been found at this cove nor Sculptor cave, which is the closer of the two to Gordonstoun. No doubt this large cave has been used for many purposes over the centuries and a torch would be handy if explored.

Gordonstoun is now the well-known private school a few miles south from the cove most noted for the unusual circular stables; it has been altered and re-designed over the centuries, and at one time, there existed hidden floors and rooms where people or perhaps smuggled contraband would have been hidden in times of trouble. Long ago during a time when even thinking the world was round was seen as blasphemous, the resident worldly laird of the time investigated the sciences within one of these hidden rooms. This later marking him as a wizard, better that than being called a witch who were being hunted and killed by the dozen within Moray at the time.

If you have no interest in exploring dark caves, viewing high cliff or the tide is in, carrying along round the cove following the narrow path via thick bushes of broom and gorse making your way to the vehicle access track to a quarry (still in use). If you did cycle this far, it would be advisable to turn right on the track and head for the main road. The path looks wide here around the quarry but later after the lookout tower, it turns narrow and nasty!

The path to the coast guard lookout tower is wide with the occasional twist and turn over ground covered with cut gorse. It could be possible to cycle this but access to the main road is easier using the quarry access road.

If the tide is out the beach can be accessed via a short scramble down the cliff to the right of the lookout tower, just follow the faint path. If the tide is in then follow the higher path leading you along the cliff edge via a narrow and often over grown path leading to a small group of houses.

Although the idea of a scramble may put you off walking along the beach, it is well worth the effort giving you access to the well-known Pict cave or more commonly known Sculptors cave. Its name is well deserved due to the half dozen engravings still visible within along with many other ones of more modern origins. The interior can be reached by two

Photo 12 –View of Timber Bridge across River Lossie.

Photo 13 – View of Lossiemouth from Sandy beach.

openings leading into a large cavern, which is surprisingly well lit, and dry. Outside the cliffs offer not only wondrous sandstone patterns like at Clashach Cove but also there are many colonies of birds, which gather upon them allowing a far more intimate view of them, then you would get along the cliff edge walk.

The cliffs slowly get lower as you near the small group of houses allowing an easier walk back up to the main path from which you could vacate to the main road by following the service track for the houses or descend down between two small stacks towards the beach. If the tide is out enough to allow access around the outcrop below the lighthouse, then you should be OK for the rest of the way to Lossiemouth (but keep an eye out for stray golf balls) or alternatively there is a faint track over the long grassy sand dunes.

There are many lighthouses around Scotland's rugged coast in some outlandish locations and you can bet your boots that the designers of them are also the ones that made the lighthouse before you. Robert Stevenson is a well-known architect and it was his son that designed Covesea skerries lighthouse, which could have also been the one he took his son to (Robert Louis Stevenson) giving him the idea for Treasure Island.

It would be nice to say that the decision to make this lighthouse was due out of safety for the local growing fishing fleet but unfortunately, it took the sinking of over 40 ships in the previous half century before it was built out of necessity and demand. The light within is automatic these days but when first opened, Lightkeepers (living in the house you have just past with their families) had to ensure that the candle was lit in all weathers. What a job that must have been!

If you like plane watching, specifically Tornadoes and other assorted fighter planes, there are two very good viewing spots in moray to catch them as they quite often go through series of landing and takeoff practice all day during week days. The first of these is while walking along the golf course section of the beach towards the large golf Hotel on the hilltop, but a much better place allowing for a family picnic are the ruins of Duffus castle situated at the other end of the runway.

Photo 14 – View of WW2 Coastal Defences from the beach.

Photo 15 – Camping amidst history.

Built at a time surrounded by the Spynie loch on a mound around mid 11th century, it now gives an excellent vantage point slightly above the surrounding farmland, with the thick walls of its keep and external walls giving kids (large and small) amble space to reenact battles of old (climbing of the walls is unadvisable due to loose masonry). During Sundays, you might also get the opportunity to see an old yellow bi-plane, which takes off from within the grounds of Gordonstoun.

Once you reach Lossiemouth, follow the road round to the Harbour, home these days to large luxurious yachts rather than a fishing fleet that are only still present in harbours further along the coast. Take time to visit the museum opposite the harbour or at least re-stock on food if you plan to wild camp by the WW2 Coastal Defences.

The long timber bridge over the River Lossie is quite visible opposite the shop, giving access to the long white sandy beach leading to Kingston. Alternatively if you are on a cycle head towards the bridge but just before crossing a small stone bridge over the Spynie Channel take the track on its right bank which will lead to the B9103. Stay on this and take the first dirt track on the left after crossing the River Lossie, this leads to a Car Park, take vehicle track on the left, then first right, left at T-junction and this will lead to the WW2 Coastal Defences and beach.

But before leaving Lossiemouth abit of history. Lossiemouth or locally known simply as 'Lossie' is quite a young town as compared to those further west having only been inhabited for the last 100 years. Up until the 18th century this area consisted of four separate villages, Old Lossie, Seatown, Branderburgh and Stotfield, all housing fisherman and their families, until the Harbour at Spynie which had serviced Elgin became too silted and a new harbour was needed. This brought about the planning of the new town Lossiemouth bringing all the villages together. The town prospered and became one of the most important harbours in the area providing shelter to many white and herring fishing boats despite a tragedy in the 19th century when a storm struck, many of which have, but with this one wiping out all but two of the towns men folk.

Apart from the fishing and the RAF base, which as of 07/2011 will be staying. A particular form of farming was carried out amongst the drained farmland surrounding the town also giving raise to the name of a great Scottish music group, RunRig.

RunRig was a form of farming that allowed the land to support a large number of tenants within a Fermtown. This Fermtown would have been a group of cottages all ran under a principal tenant or 'tackman'. Each of these would have had a garden to grow their own vegetables and keep livestock as well as a strip of land 200 x 40 feet wide (the Run) upon which they grew a crop to sell, each separated from one another by a ditch (The Rig). Initially this was seen as a good system and could be extended as families grew but eventually over the years, the constant use of the soil for growing wore it out.

Stage 3 – **WW 2 Coastal Defences to Kingston** – OS sheet 28, 424

Distance – 3.4 miles   Height gain/loss – 16m/0m

One second the wind was howling constantly shifting and bulging the fat dark clouds above, until suddenly the sun appeared, radiant and strong chasing the clouds and wind away coating him in a blanket of warmth, and safety. The sea before him now calmer sparkled like a bed of fine cut diamonds upon gentle rolling waves.

He heard his name being called, at first distant and dim, growing louder and louder and.........

'Private, wake up and get ready to stand to'

A dream...as he sat up the sun was nowhere, in fact, it was dark, cold, and wet – another day had started guarding the coast of Moray.

Given Morays past history of being invaded by one race or another it is hardly surprising, why in the 1940's that its low sandy beaches from Findhorn to Kingston were seen as ideal landing zones, a reason also why it was used for practice for the D-Day landings.

To deter the Germans from landing, huge amounts of Pillboxes and concrete blocks were made and installed along these beaches, many of which from Lossiemouth to Kingston are still in tiptop condition and showing signs of residence. With the glowing glory of all these defences being, the batteries and associate buildings present at this location. Both Polish and Welsh regiments were involved in the construction of the main battery defences which were then mostly manned by Home Guard forces. As you look around the defences and perhaps stay the night, images of Mainwaring at his men running around working the WW1 naval guns make you wonder how it would have fared if the guns had ever been used.

From here carry on down the pebbled track towards Kingston or perhaps venture over to the shoreline. Whichever you choose keep your eyes out for the many plants along the path such as bell heather plus countless mosses, and not forgetting birds, the sandpiper in particular who has a knack of staying just out of zoom range unless you have a digital or film SLR camera.

Eventually upon reaching the shooting range you encounter vehicle tracks, there are signs here leading to an alternative route via bin hill but the route is not marked and involves narrow over grown paths and best left unless you'd like to see the range. A strange sight with its 600m of well kept undulating grass amongst the surrounding stones and tree's.

The line of pillboxes and concrete blocks finish at this point and if you climb the lookout post adjacent to the start of the firing range you can clearly see the long line of defences fading into the distance unlike the reason for their creation and use.

These defences are of stone but far more memorable is the defence in war time offered by the hordes of fisherman from the many ports of Moray. Not only did they still fish to help prevent the U-boats attempt to starve the UK but on many occasions they were brought into service by the Royal navy during both world wars for boom defence , act as convoy escorts, plus swept the north sea for mines and as part of anti submarine patrols. Some used their own boats, others boats which the admiralty built and later gave to them after the war.

Some of these men could have very well come from Kingston, used to the rigors of work at sea from an early age, perhaps starting their career as young as 12 or 14 in merchant navy possibly reaching the rank of Master 6 years later. Alternatively, he could have followed in his father footsteps and become a fisherman or bait man going to sea clothed in thick canvas coated in oil, eating dull food and experiencing fierce storms aboard a small boat to lay long lines of hooks for herring or haddock, previously baited by his kids and wife earlier in the day. The fish he caught would then been gutted and salted by the wife.

Curiously one of Morays most renowned dishes comes from haddock and the locals skill at smoking fish, this being a type of Skink (soup or stew). Traditionally cooked with beef, most people could not afford that and used the most readily available as a substitute; I.e. smoked haddock. It is called Cullen Skink from the village where it was devised and can be sampled in most places within moray although the recipe does tend to differ from place to place.

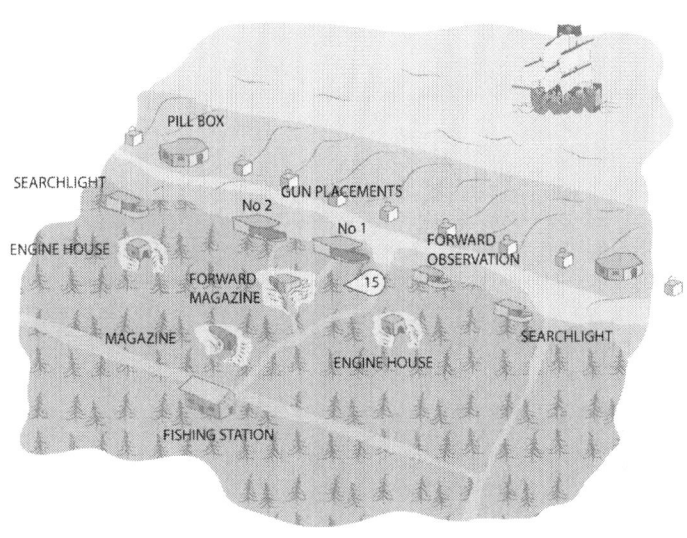

Figure 12 – Plan of Lossiemouth Coastal defence Battery.

Photo – 16 – Perfect line of concrete blocks looking towards Kingston.

In Kingston and Garmouth, those left at home would have equally felt vulnerable to not only the perils at sea and the possibility of being made a widow or fatherless in times when government benefits and pensions were a dream for the future, but also from the shifting mouth of the River Spey threatening at times to sweep away houses. It was not uncommon to wake and see the river just outside and other times a mile away.

The Kingston of today has no such worries with the local Moray council periodically digging out the silt built up within the main channel serving to ensure in some small part that it mouth stays put. The small compact white buildings you pass by now may not be resident to fisherman and their families but they still look the part with the strong smell of salt water in the air.

Kingston to Fochabers

Distance – 5 miles   Height gain/loss – 14m/0m

Following the road out of Kingston will take you directly to Garmouth. Alternatively, you could take the first narrow lane on the right along the entrance to Kingston, which leads to a narrow path across the crest of a hill offering excellent views of the River Spey mouth and the picturesque Viaduct you will be crossing. Once within Garmouth follow the road up past the small local shop taking the first left which leads to the short descent onto the disused railway track on your left taking you over the River Spey via the luxury of the viaduct amidst an array of colourful blooms if walked in spring and through woods of alder.

Originally called Garmouth Harbour, it is hard to believe that Garmouth was an important harbour at one time, now so far from the riverbank, for the fishing trade as well as for ship builders where shipwrights from England build vessels of up to 500 tons during the 18th century. But Centuries before, this areas fame started on a beautiful day in June 1650 when a royal visitor came to Garmouth, namely Charles II from his exile in Holland during the Civil War. After hearing of his fathers demise, he was sought out to aid and uphold the Covenant and after a long journey, during which they had to try and not be spotted by Cromwell's fleet, finally arrived off shore.

Photo 17 – Looking North along Vehicle track access to Range

Photo 18 – Looking toward Kingston from hill top

However, the era's historical and political facts are not what are important, it is more the way he came to shore. It was certainly not to a fanfare of streamers and cheers from the harbour because the Dutch man of War could not get there. The man of War anchor at the mouth of the River Spey from where he got passage for part of the way on one of her boats, for the remainder a local ferryman called Milne carried him piggyback style to the shoreline.

The spot where the king came ashore is where Kingston is now, at that time the town did not exist. Only later in early 18th Century was Kingston created due to extra harbour space needed closer to the sea, its name coming not from the royal piggyback but from the shipwrights who came and named the village after Kingston on the River Humber.

The Fertile flat lands or Laich o' Moray may have been the cause of Morays importance to a succession of invaders and settlers but the River Spey was also important in the past creating a huge industry around the building of merchant and naval ships. Second largest and fastest flowing river in Scotland it was only bridged in the early 18th Century posing a huge barrier to all that needed passage over it, but for a means of transporting timber from the vast forest that once covered the entire length of it especially around the Rothiemurchus and Abernethy areas, it was perfect.

These Forests had been harvested since the arrival of the first settlers, mostly to clear land for farming but when the naval and merchant powers of UK sailed the four corners of the world in timber boats the forest of inland Moray were cut down in earnest especially when the railroad was built allowing for faster land transportation. For this reason the harbours around the mouth were very busy seeing some of the highest numbers of ships being built and new designs developed during the 18th and 19th century.

That is all gone now, the river and its banks being turned over more to the preservation and observation of its natural wonders including Dolphins beyond the River Spey Mouth. This can be investigated more if you turn left once over the viaduct to follow The Moray Coastal Trail to the visitor centre just a mile away. For the Moray way, turn right following the rough vehicle track along the edge of the alder woods.

Photo 19 – Steps leading down from road to the Viaduct

Photo 20 – The viaduct crossing

Thus far, this route has been over sand and roads with little evidence of the Laich o' Moray fertile land so often spoke about. From here on in your are going to see plenty of it over tracks like the one you're on, narrow paths, some roads again but mostly along the way you will encounter the infamous boggy ground so often remarked about, more so in wet weather. You will also encounter deviations from the main route, the first of these about 1 ½ miles along this track where the erosion of the River Spey has literally swept the track away to sea.

Standing near the edge of where the track disappears, it may seem amazing how so much land could be just swept away in so short a time, and not even marked on maps yet. If the River is in spate then you're probably see why but imagine if you had to cruise down it as part of a job. Hilarious for some no doubt but before the 18th Century and the industrial age there were no roads like today only perhaps narrow paths giving access along the River Spey to the coast. In those days, the only way the timber, so important for shipping was transported down river was on it, sometimes up to 20,000 logs a day.

First the cut logs were thrown into the river, this being the job for only the strongest and giving rise to the sport of 'Tossing the caber' at Highland Games. Next these logs were guided down river by men on the banks with long poles who funny enough got 'a competent allowance of spirituous liquor' as well as 1s 2d a day but this method had flaws culminating in many logs being lost out to sea.

To help prevent this from happening a man called Aaron Hill came up with the idea of making the logs into rafts by means of drilling holes in the ends of the logs, driving in iron rods with eyes enabling each log to be tied together with wattles (twisted branches). Upon these rafts men, said to be mostly Grants guided them down the River Spey. Despite most large rocks and other potential obstacles having been cleared out of the way, you can imagine the dangers involved in this job and as well as being paid more, the allowance of liquor must have been double at least.

Leaving the River behind, take the detour on the left over a narrow path along the edge of the woods until entering it on the right taking you to a much more rugged path over exposed roots and tree stumps, where Cyclists will have to carry or push their bikes for about 200m until rejoining the vehicle tracks. Turn left at the junction of tracks where your lead through a pine wood heading nearer to the main road, then turn

Photo 21 – Erosion of the Moray way

Photo 22 – Narrow path through a woodland of alder and birch.

right and take the narrow path just before the river on the left. This paths leads directly to Fochabers taking you under the two bridges of the A96 and Railway line via a very nice stretch of birch and alder woodland, whose floor in spring is covered in wood sorrel.

Apart from this areas shipping history, there is a name nearby on the map involving a part of Morays history, which is hotly debated, this being 'Roman Camp Gate'. No evidence exists to suggest that this was a Roman camp, but recent finds of Roman coin hordes from Birnie (NJ21058) and Clarkly hill above Burghead. Some from differing time periods, suggest that Romans did indeed either need to bribe for peace or purchase items from the local Pict, perhaps both!

Nearly everything involving the Romans around this part of Scotland has a big question mark upon it. The battle of Mons Graupius (from which the Grampian Mountains got their name) certainly happened, but where exactly. The Romans had a large naval fleet, which circumnavigated around Scotland, Ptolemy's map and Tacitus (Agricola's son in law) accounts of the battle prove this. But, why would the Romans need to pay the local tribes. There are suggestions that they mined for iron ore along the Moray coast at Cullen and Portsoy, which they needed for their huge war machine and constant need for armour and swords, or the Romans did export bears from Scotland (not extinct in Scotland until circa 1000AD) was it payment for them?

Sometimes history can be a very interesting subject, especially where question marks hang upon it. The archeologists from the national museum of Scotland have only just started their digging at Clarkly hill and it will be interesting to see what they unearth.

Stage 4 – **Fochabers to Boat O'Brig** – OS sheet 28, 424

Distance – 3.4 miles   Height gain/loss – 119m/100m

Fochabers like many of the towns around Moray started around a prominent point, in Fochabers case this was Gordon Castle but as the population grew, a new location for the growing town was sought during a stage in Scottish history when it was seen as fashionable for landowners to create new villages. Hence its present location and having been marshy ground at the time, gave rise to its name (originally called *Fothopir – Foth* for land and *Opir* for a marsh, bog or fen).

The modern bridge across River Spey was built quite recently, the original built by Thomas Telford in the 19th Century. Before this a ford at Birnie (near roman gate) was used by Edward I and his huge Army on his way to 'Bon Chastell' (Elgin castle on lady Hill), plus ferries may have operated as they did at Boat O'Brig serving customers using the great Kings High way from Inverness to Aberdeen.

The town was designed in a grid fashion with narrow streets and close-knit houses similar to most new towns. A design feature which may have been a hangover from older towns like Forres, whose narrow streets were primarily designed to make it difficult for roving bands of highlanders and 'Outlanders' who at one time used to raid towns now and again.

The town may have had one or two wells built to provide fresh water before the advent of pipes and taps, and a tollhouse would have been built alongside the king's high way. Going by the presence of the local name 'Auchenhalrig' Fochabers would have certainly had a slaughterhouse. The name meaning 'field of the deer traps' where the deer would have been driven into and killed as they fled through a narrow gap at the head of a small glen. In addition, they may have had a local hill at one time called locally 'Cnoc na Croiche' meaning the hill of the gallows where local criminals would have been hung. However, they were not alone in this respect as most towns had one. Perhaps not the most savoring fact to hear about as you enter Fochabers, but most of these hills are long gone with only a few remaining on maps only!

After leaving the bridges behind, the path widens underneath a short stretch of woodland leading to a level open space. Make your way to the gravel track on your left and upon reaching the memorial garden further on take some time to read the names of the famous people of Fochabers, which are listed on two stone slabs. Two exquisite flowerbeds surround these slabs and the view between the slabs of the wide and calm River Spey beyond make this point ideal to take a breather for awhile, if only to read the names of Fochaberians who spanned the world as successful scientist, business men and soldiers.

From the memorial following the track to a small stream heading on its way to the river and take the gravel track to the left of it leading up into the village. Follow this until the second bridge or alternatively take the second road on the left leading to the village square and shops.

Across the bridge, carry straight on past the school on the left and head for the farm gate across the small round about. At a crossroad of tracks, the normal route is to carry straight on through a narrow section wood to the road out of Fochabers. But if you're a Cyclists and would like to gain access to the Moray Monster trails, turn left at the crossroads, right on the road and the car park is just as you enter Castle Hill woods on the left.

For those who do not know, Moray Monster trails are a series of long and short, easy to darn right terrifying cycle trails built within the Wood of Ordiequish and the woods surrounding Ben Aigan (471m) stretching for the entire distance of this section. Most of the moderate (Blue) trails can be accessed from this car park such as the 'Haggis' and 'Soup Dragon' or even the severe (Black) 'Gully Monster'. You could even use the Haggis to gain access to the predominantly difficult (Red) trails under Ben Aigan making your way to Craigellachie all within woods exiting from the 'Ben Aigan Hammer' or better the 'Bunny' which follows the Moray Way route for part of it.

Although the highest point along this route is at Dava moor, this section has the accolade of having the highest amount of descending and ascending. Basically after reaching the top of one point, you get a nice clear run down until you have to climb again. This will happen quite a few times, for Cyclists it means a series of joy rides down steep inclines over tarmac and forest tracks but walkers will enjoy the many viewpoints along this route of the Spey valley. The first being a few miles from the Monster trail car park up the gradual climb of the road.

Photo 23 – View from Fochabers of the River Spey

Photo 24 – Looking back down the ravine

It comes with the unusual name of Earth Pillers vantage point, and serves best at showing a last glimpse of the coast revealing also the growing height of the hills bordering the River Spey. Next comes a steep decline down to a deep ravine caused by the Burn of Aultderg, unfortunately there is a sharp left bend at the bottom followed by another before a steep ascent leading you out of the ravine. OK for walkers but takes all the forward motion advantage away plus meaning your need to be in a low gear as the ascent is steep from the start.

The rest of the journey to Boat O'Brig follows a much easier gradient with the occasional climb until just before when there is another steep ascent with bends but not as sharp as in the ravine. It is a gentle part of the walk offering occasional views of the River Spey glen on your right when out of the trees of the heather covered hills down through the woods skirting along the banks of the wide fast flowing River Spey.

The River Spey has during its long human history been of the most valuable resource to this county, providing a means of easy transport, offered fruits of its fish and whisky from its unique properties, but it has also taken quite a lot from it as well, and still does. This brought about the Moray alleviation scheme costing 86 million so far, where long lines of embankments are built along main rivers and around major towns to help stop the reoccurrence of the damage which the River Spey along with the River Findhorn, Nairn and Lossie rivers can do.

In living history, there have been many floods, which have devastated homes and business, but it is the great flood of 1829, which stirs the most fear of what these rivers together can do. It happened in August during a summer, which had been noted for being very dry until the night of the 1st when a dark cloud appeared over the Moray Firth, growing in size and darkness until it reached the Monadliath mountains.

All these rivers spring from these mountains and the sheets and torrents of rain, which poured from the dark cloud swept down all of them as if a dam had been broken, sweeping everything in its path along with it. Homes, animals, tree's, bridges, the sounds it made were reported to be like continuous cannon fire. For three days the rain poured, the River Spey reaching the foothills of its glen and the River Findhorn reaching heights of 50 feet above its normal level. Along the coast thunderous waves added to the fear of the populace and with the floods, coming towards the sea it

Photo 25 – Looking east past Boat O'Brig

Photo 26 – Looking west along the River Spey

must have seemed to the locals that there was nowhere to escape this deluge. On the morning of the fourth day the storms had past, the populace woke to roam a devastated land, and a coastline dotted with its victims.

Most of the rain normally comes from the west, the clouds following the prominent winds dropping their contents as they travel over the western highlands and finally the Monadliath. In the case of the great storm they had some warning of impending danger but it is not uncommon to come across rivers in the lowlands that are full to bursting even during dry spells, it is not the sunshine above which matters most but the clouds over the rivers source that does.

On the brighter side of the River Spey in particular, the length you are walking along from Fochabers to Arndilly (just before Craigellachie) represents the lower stage of the river fishing beats. The upper goes from Aviemore to Grantown on Spey, the middle from Castle Grant to Craigellachie. Any fishermen worth his salt has no doubt stood amidst the currents of this or any river in Moray and along this lower stage you have to feel sorry for the salmon. As if they did not have enough obstacles and a current to get over or through but if the local adage about the River Spey is believed then this stage has the potential of the most catches of salmon during day and trout at night;

February to March – Brea to Delfur

April to June – Delfur/Rothes to Tulchan

July to August – level spread

September - From Orton to sea.

Delfur to Arndilly is regarded as the 'Holy land' by Spey anglers as this location offers the most constant catches. Also a location made famous by John Ashley Cooper who once nearly caught a 50lb salmon along this stretch. Many beats exist along each stage, each with Ghillies, a hut and perhaps a boat from which to sample the many pools or just wade out over the wide expanse on stone and pebbles, feeling the current wrap around you, leaving you alone except for the summer insects and

Photo 27 – Narrow Forest track

Photo 28 – Wide firm Forest track

perhaps one or two other fly-fishers on this wide river. The possibilities of catching 20 fish before lunch may not exist anymore as they did during the rivers heyday of the 1950 to 1960's, but the joy of fishing on one of the worlds supreme salmon rivers still does.

Boat O'Brig to Craigellachie

Distance – 9.1 miles   Height gain/loss – 250m/224m

At the end of the road from Fochabers, you go under the Railway and join the B9103. There is a small Car Park on your right offering a chance of a breather under the shade of trees before moving on. The route from here is to take the short stretch of steps up the hill just before the tollhouse building on the left to join a rough track that takes you up to and around an old dis used building. From there a straight vehicle track takes you to the entrance of the forest. Alternatively, you could cycle up the B9103 avoiding the rough tracks and join the straight vehicle track 1km away on the right but this road is used often by the large trucks coming out of the local distillery and being narrow could pose danger.

You are now entering the woods under Ben Aigan (471m) and are going to walk/cycle around on one of its steep sides; to begin with, the track is narrow and can be over grown and wet. However, after a steep climb this track leads to wide firm graveled track. The going is good over this ground but three rivers coming off the Ben have created four small ravines, each of these involving a climb and fall. Similar to but more severe than those along the earlier road route, they are great for Cyclists, especially the last continuing down to the road. For walkers they offer some of the best views of the day taking you to the highest point along the River Spey that this route reaches, just under 300m. The best of these would be at the top of the first and second climb, off back towards the River Spey mouth. There are also some views on offer towards the old distillery town of Rothes but only glimpses through the pine trees as you descend towards the road at Arndilly.

What is on offer in abundance during this stage is the opportunity to see some wildlife. On bike, this could be very difficult but during the slow

Photo 29 – From Campsite in Craigellachie towards pub

Photo 30 – View left of campsite

process of hiking, you may get the odd glimpse of movement. Red squirrels abound throughout Moray, grays are here as well but it seems that they have not totally chased the reds away from what is one of their last few locations. Early morning or dusk is perhaps the best times to see the reds. But don't be surprised if you're quiet enough to get a whisper of movement out of the corner of your eye during any time of the day to see one of these fast small fury animals perform a series of acrobatics as it scampers up and down the tree's, its movements fast, yet in tune with the environment.

Birds of prey are often seen, sometimes in the most unlikely of places like along roads resting on a post, especially the buzzard that is common in these parts. Plus keep a look out for deer as you wander along. More than likely it will be the small roe deer your see alone or part of a group either grazing lower than you amidst the pine or jumping over the track, always too fast for the camera. It is very unlikely to see red deer this low in summer having plenty of grazing available up on the moors but there are farms in Moray, which breed them for the venison like cows for milk or beef.

These deer are unlikely to gain the prestige of becoming a stag; even wild deer only earn that upon their fifth year. During their first year they are known as a 'Knobber', in the second a 'Brocket'. In the third year they develop brow antlers and are known as 'Spayard', in the fourth year they acquire bay antlers and the name 'Staggard'. Then comes the fifth year and the growth of royal antlers earning them the name of 'Stag'. But to gain the ultimate name of 'Royal Stag', they would have to have survived not only the savagery of several Scottish winters, fights with other stags during the ruts of Autumn, diseases, and constant harassment from Midges but also a royal hunt. No wonder they stand mightily and strong upon the high ridges after combating all that.

After the nice ride or walk down out of the pinewoods, you reach a one lane tarmac road mostly used by the local farmers. This leads all the way to Craigellachie under the canopy of beech whose floor is once again coated in wood sorrel during early spring. There are fields along it where the Scottish cowe graze and a couple of bridges you pass over made from old iron that might be of interest to some, but more than likely after the last stage it is the Fiddochside Inn your more interested in seeing.

It is a very small affair situated on the banks of the Fiddich, so influential on the areas whiskies and available to drink within. It has been in the same family for decades, unfortunately serves no food, but the benches outside allow you to relax and sip your drink overlooking the river and a well kept garden. From the pub, the free camping spot is directly opposite and access across the river taking the first path or track on the left.

Stage 5 – **Craigellachie to Carron** – OS sheet 28, 424, 419

Distance – 6 miles   Height gain/loss – 34m/0m

Tell them wha hae the chief direction
Scotland an' me's in great affliction,
E'er sin' they laid that curst restriction
On aqua-vitae;
An' rouse them up to strong conviction,
An' move their pity

Scotland, my auld, respected mither!
Tho' whiles ye moistify your leather,
Till whare ye sit on craps o' heather
Ye tine your dam,
Freedom and whisky gang thegither,
Taka ff your dram!

Two verses from the poem 'The Authors Earnest Cry and Prayer' by Robert Burns

If you have partaken in some of the fine whiskeys from the Fiddochside Inn or stayed in the old style, luxurious comfort of Highland Inn with its range of 280 different blends as well as some from abroad. You may not be in the mood for a poem, definitely not a walk, but perhaps a short history about the local whisky and its origins would be OK. For Mr. Colt may have made all men equal but it took the Scots to make them all joyfully intoxicated.

Traditionally, Scotland's whisky production is split into four area's; The Highlands, The Lowlands, Islands (including Campbeltown) and finally Speyside, which contains almost half of the countries distilleries, partly due to the areas abundance of the raw material needed and the sweetest peaty water within her rivers. Economically and spiritually Scottish whisky has lived up to it name for centuries; Uisage Beatha, meaning the 'Water of Life' from which the word 'Whiskey is derived from.

If you wish to know more about these distilleries, experience their smells and share in the angels portion, plus thrill your taste buds with free samples, then the Whiskey trail is the perfect means to visit working distilleries and the cooperage where all the barrels are made, but more importantly, your learn the secrets of their double and single malts. A secret, which arrived here in the 9th century from either the Celts who picked it up as they travelled through Europe or from Monks whose knowledge and creation of herbal brews and tinctures, lent them also to be the innovators of Ales and Beers as herbal remedies.

Before Robert Burns (1759 – 1796) was born, there were already a few legal distilleries, as well as illicit ones. Then taxes on Whisky were raised steeply after the union of the Scottish and English Parliament in 1707, to try to discourage illicit stills when all it did was create many more. In some areas to extreme amounts, over 400 alone within the wild and desolates hills of Glenlivet, the antics and tales of which are discussed within 'The Detail' of the Ben Macdui trail, along with the cat and mouse game they played constantly with the local Gaugers or Tax Collectors.

As the area became more open and accessible with the building of roads and rail, the Gaugers became more intensive, causing many of these illicit stills to decline. Some of these illicit brewers deciding instead to open legal distilleries, with many of the Distilleries surviving today having such beginnings.

From the free campsite follow the wide track under the road bridge as it leads you around the edge of the town, under the A941 and then the A95 bringing you out into the open from where you get your first glimpse of the oldest surviving cast iron arched bridge in Scotland.

Designed by Thomas Telford, it will be 200 years old in 2014 and owes its survival to the initiative of local engineers who knowing the levels this river could reach during floods, advised Telford to raise it by five feet.

This stage of the route from Craigellachie to Cragganmore is quite different to the last, in comparison it could be called serene and relaxing. For the majority of its length it takes you over the gentle gradient of a disused rail path, sometimes wide like from this point to Aberlour,

Photo31 – View from under A95 to Craigellachie Bridge

Photo 32 – Track towards Aberlour

sometimes over grown like between Aberlour and Carron. Never far from the river and constantly in and out of woods and farmland giving a real mixture of low-level scenery and ample more opportunities to spot wildlife and plants along the verge.

The track turns to a well kept path as you enter Aberlour on the river side leading to a well kept park. The path divides here joining again after the park. The left leading towards the town giving access to its square and shops with the right hugging the river and from where you get a real sense of the River Spey's worth to fly fishermen and the community at large. As you witness the ritual of tons of rainwater flow fast and easy downstream, what better view could you get but from the narrow suspension bridge just along the bank from where you can get a real appreciation of the rivers power and width.

Aberlour as a town was created for the same reason as Fochabers, but this time by the Grants who wished to collect all manner of mechanics and tradesman into a small area. At one point, the population of the town was very high for the area due an orphanage built here to house Children from all over Scotland, but after this closed down the population dropped dramatically. These days the town is most famous for the production of Walkers shortbread started by two brothers who hailed from the Glenlivet area.

After the park the two paths rejoin again just before a narrow wooden bridge. The left path leads straight towards it, access from the right is after the suspension bridge over a small bridge then left up past a wood. Across the bridge, the path is very rough for awhile but opens out and levels just before you start a gentle decline within woods.

The rail track you are following was part of the Strathspey railway with this line being a spur between Craigellachie and Boat of Garten, just one small part of 'The great north of Scotland Railway' or 'Gnsr' for short. It was opened in 1863 and serviced the distilleries and local communities for just over 100 years before it was closed due to rail cuts when transport by road was seen as much cheaper. All of the rail tracks along this route were created at much the same time during the early days of steam transport when horses were still used on the roads and cars were unheard of.

Photo 33 – Track from suspension bridge

Photo 34 – Narrow Bridge where the park paths rejoin

The sight, sound and smells of steam crisscrossed Moray over these hundred years and would have been responsible for opening up Moray to the greater world, which up to this time was regarded as still remote or out of reach to most folk. Thankfully, due to volunteers and a lot of hard work this joy that is steam can still be enjoyed locally at the Strathspey Steam Railway, which runs between Aviemore and Boat of Garten on a 10-mile stretch of the old Inverness and Perth junction Railway.

Nowadays the only remnants of this railway left are countless bridges, small stone ones like the one you will pass under further along the incline from Aberlour and later you will see more examples of cast iron latticed bridges over the River Spey. Along this stage you will also notice old fire hearths set back within a retaining wall, which only seem to exist on the section between Aberlour and Carron.

The incline slowly levels out as you enter fields before descending back into the woods past the Treatment Plant, which cleans effluent from all the distilleries before returning it back into the River Spey. Past the plant you will join its access road for a short time before it turns uphill and you pass by the first of many old rail platforms.

This platform is certainly a strange sight to see, it is well kept, still has some signs and park benches giving it a still in use feel and if you decide to rest on the benches you will not be forgiven in the feeling of expecting a train to arrive at any time.

After leaving the platform, you will start to get the definite smell of whisky distillering and the aromatic smell of malt, some will hate it, some will love it, nevertheless, it just a sign that you are getting near to Carron. Cross over the road or join it and cross over the Bridge. This one is quite wide but has one side shut off to road traffic allowing you time to soak in the views of the spey below in peace although to view the quaint fishing hut on the right side you will need to watch out.

Follow the road into the small and quiet town of Carron, taking the first left or using the path past the red telephone box, then take the first right leading you past the Distillery on the left and woods on the right.

Carron Distillery was built for Imperial established by Thomas Mackenzie in 1897 after the railway was built when other distilleries were also expanding. It is said that due to its large stills that it could make either large quantities of whisky or none at all and has gone through a

Photo 35 – State of track after decline from fields

Photo 36 – State of track after the Treatment Plant

series of closures and re ownership. As of 2005, Pernod Ricard (formally Chivas Brothers) operates it.

Carron to Cragganmore

Distance – 5.1 miles   Height gain/loss – 32m/0m

Just as you pass the Distillery buildings, the Moray Way path veers off to the left of the single lane road, staying level with it until the two part company by a new looking house on the left. From here, you are back onto the rail track and straight into the woods. After a mile the track takes on a slow curve to the left with Knockando House on the right as your cross over a picturesque river. The house will be out of view along with the River Spey but from this point the river starts a series of sharp twists and bends where it roars louder than before as the peaty waters are forced over rocks and between high banks until after Knockando where the river becomes gentle again on its way to Cragganmore.

In spring the track can be quite open, dry and easily travelled along, where as during summer, the rains can turn it into an overgrown marsh in places. Still very navigational but the occasional Nettle hanging over will need to be avoided plus perhaps the Indian Balsam with its unique flowers, with the Spear Thistle putting in an appearance now and again as well as the fragrance of the Meadow Sweet and Willow herb. Smaller flowers include the Self heal, so called because of its abilities to aid in many ailments, speedwell, the wood sorrel is especially common, pansy and within the wetter verges, the weird looking Mares Tail looking like some left over from pre historic woodlands.

Of course, not all these plants put in an appearance along the whole of the River Spey. As you travel along it, you will notice subtle changes in the undergrowth as you near Grantown on Spey with each season also adding to the variety with not only the plants and trees around you but also the river. In spring the level is quite constant as melt waters from the mountains consistently flows where as during July/August periodic heavy rain falls can put the level up to record-breaking heights with autumn seeing the calmest time.

During Sundays when fishing is not allowed (season from 11th February till 3oth September) apart from the sounds of birds and the movement of the trees you might also hear laughter or other associated noises

Photo 37 – View from Road Bridge to Carron

Photo 38 – View of track on long stretch to Cragganmor

humans make while canoeing. The distance between Cragganmore and the road bridge over to Carron being a popular stretch for organized trips although the swift adventurous canoeist might be spotted at any point along its length, quite different to the more common motionless quiet fly fisherman present during the rest of the week.

In line with the course of the river, the track follows suit bending next to the right where you are brought close to the Tamdhu Distillery where you might catch the distinctive aroma of malted barley because unlike any other distillery, Highland Distilleries Ltd (the present owners) Malt their own Barley on the premises. Created in 1897, Tamdhu means 'Little Dark Hill' and is a major component of the 'Famous Grouse' whisky brand.

Just down the track, avoiding the landslide, you arrive at the old Knockando railway Station that is now the visitor centre for Tamdhu. From here you can rest and get some great vantage points over the River Spey along this particular bend in it and perhaps see some canoeist or especially the rich woodlands both sides of it.

After the station the path leads you past another working Distillery, that of Knockando Distillery (owned by Diageo, formally Guinness PLC). Started a year later then Tamdhu its name means 'little black hill' and can be sampled as a single malt or just might be detected within J & B Blends.

Past the distillery, you enter a section with prominent views over fields to the river with periodic lengths of woodland remaining like this to Cragganmore. There is another bridge over a river and you will encounter many farm gates that will not need Cyclists to dismount and open as they provide an opening around them.

Next comes the old station which is Blackboat, it does offer a place to camp but can be overgrown and does not provide toilets which the free campsite at Cragganmore does. Unlike the previous station which served mostly the interest of the distilleries, this station was for the locals and did have two platforms. Since closing in 1965, the riverside platform has been removed as well as the rail tracks but the main building looks in very good condition.

Photo 39 – Bridge over river after Knockando

Photo 40 – Blacksboat Station

The rest of the route to Cragganmore is easy going with only a narrow bridge offering some difficulty to Cyclists who will have to dismount and push the bike over. After this the tracks runs parallel to the B9102 for a while then heads straight towards a cast iron bridge over the river into Cragganmore.

Photo 41 – Narrow Bridge just before River Spey

Photo 42 – Cast Iron Bridge over to Cragganmore

Stage 6 – Cragganmore to Mains of Dalvey, OS sheet 28, 36, 419, 418

Distance – 4.3 miles Height gain/loss – 199m/162m

The henchman and the laird rested easy beside a warming fire from the surrounding night beside the beginnings of a majestic castle. They were waiting for something to happen, what this was they did not know but tonight all would be answered.

Then slowly the soft breeze and easy feeling started to wane as a strong wind could be heard coming from the coast, at first nothing more but a strong wind, then turning into a whirlwind of dark menace thrashing and bending the trunks of Oaks surrounding the men and the castle. Its stone walls withstood this initial onslaught but then the odd brick started to fly through the air upon a great roar and devilish speed of the wind. The two men could do nothing as they too were swept away over the cliff down down to the banks of the River Avon, and certain death only halted by the stout branches of a tree upon which they were trapped waiting for the nightmare to stop, then in the peace of the aftermath they heard the ghostly wind speak

'Build it on the cow haugh'

So states the legend of Ballindalloch castle and the reason for its present location. Originally, the local Laird had wanted it built on a rise called 'The Castle Stripe' giving it the defensive advantage of overlooking the surrounding Glen Spey, and in present times making it visible from the cast iron bridge into Cragganmore. However, dark forces had other ideas and for the two proceeding nights before the laird vigilant watch strange whirlwind had ripped the castle walls apart witnessed by the superstitious workers.

The laird needed to see what or who was responsible for this outraged convinced that it was merely the work of an angry neighbor. He certainly got his answer plus a prompt of where to build it, being now its present location. Unfortunately, this location does mean that it cannot be viewed any other way than driving down the castle access. If you have the time, it is well worth the admission fee to see a castle or manor house unlike any other in Moray whose elegance, pure architectural wonder and majestic gardens are unforgettable, not counting the historical contents the castle walls of the Macpherson-Grants.

After the cast iron bridge the track becomes rougher over gravel taking past the small settlement of Cragganmore of unique log cabins and modern stone houses. The free campsite is just before the old run down station building accessed through a gate underneath a thick canopy of trees. Between the campsite and the station is the road, turn left to carry along The Speyside Way spur to Tomintoul (covered on that leg of the BMT), right takes you to one of the oldest distilleries in this area.

John Smith a man referred to locally at the time as 'The Giant' founded Cragganmore Distillery in 1869, well known already for the success he had achieved at other distilleries. Presently it is owned by Diageo (formally Guinness PLC) and produces a distinctive single malt whose unique flavor is achieved by using flat-topped spirit stills, the vapors from which condense in wooden worm tubs.

Past the station, the track continues on gravel through a birch wood until you have to descend a few steps to cross a tarmac road rejoining the track via a short slope. From here the track becomes smoother but with exposed roots in places.

Up until this point, the route has been very easy, just a matter of following the rail track but shortly after the road crossing the route takes on a much different character where you are taken away from the track over narrow boggy paths through farmland, woods and moorland until the Mains of Dalvey, the route is well sign posted. If you were cycling then it would be easier to turn left at the Cragganmore station and follow the A95 to the mains.

The choice is yours depending if you think the following route is worth taking your bike over or not. The A95 from the turning into Cragganmore to where the paths joins it is steep containing a few bends but most importantly it is the main artery for all traffic within the Elgin area and the A9 to southern Scotland and offers few overtaking opportunities for vehicles.

Photo 43 – Track beyond Cragganmore

Photo 44 – Narrow path between track and A95

Along this part of the Moray Way, you will start to encounter an access gate, which resembles and operates like a guillotine (see photo 45). Easy to open but as soon as you let go of each side, they swing back potentially catching your rear foot before it has cleared it, so walkers are best to side step like a crab. It is possible to get bikes through it but demands care and in some places these gates occur quite often especially towards the end of the first part as you near the A95 just past Tormore Distillery.

The reason for this change becomes clear by the sudden appearance of a high fence across the track leading up the hill along which you follow for a while. Signs on the fence indicating that the area beyond is used to raise Pheasant. The plus side to this change is that after quite a few miles of the confines along the track from woodland and the high sides of the glen is that you will once again start to get views of the surrounding countryside. Cyclists would have covered the distance quite quickly but walkers may now appreciate a change in surroundings just like during stage 4, you will be lead higher up the hill side via different environments offering a change in the wildlife and flora spotting potential finally reaching the domain of the heather if only for awhile. The first view being one of the youngest distilleries in the area that of Tormore built in 1958. the appearance of the buildings are another of the locals architectural wonders topped off perfectly by the ornamental trees and bushes visible from the road side. It is available as a single malt or blended in with 'Long John'.

The path up from the track is narrow, steep and covered in exposed roots during the short steep climb through sparse woodland of birch. Upon obtaining the level, you enter farmland with much of your route fenced in guiding you to the right and over a section of boggy ground where large slabs have been placed to keep you from sinking into it. This brings you to the narrow path as shown in photo 44 and the start of the gates. Follow this round leading you over many gates past the farmland, and then through a woodland where the path can become very overgrown finally leading to a very rough farm track. This takes you to the A95.

Unless you have heavy panniers on your cycle, some Cyclists may have opted to take this path to avoid a tricky part of the A95, from this point the road is straight with gentle curving corners and mainly downhill

Photo 45 – The Guillotine gate

Photo 46 – Forest track ascended to from A95

leveling out beside the river. It still has no verge to escape the larger vehicles but they can at least see far enough ahead to overtake you in places. Follow this past the traffic lights and take the next turning on the left for the Mains of Dalvey.

For walkers and Cyclists who love a sense of adventure off the beaten track and do not mind carrying their bike over another 25 odd gates then cross the A95 and follow the faint path on the left side.

After awhile the path turns 90 degrees up the hill between young birch and an assortment of broom and gorse bushes with small birds and many flying insects keeping you company as well as the occasional pheasant until you reach the pinewoods. Climb over the stile and take the narrow path leading up to the forest track shown in photo 46.

For Cyclists this track does not offer much rest from pushing the bike as directly after the climb the Moray Way goes back into the pinewoods. At first the descent is gradual but leads to a walk straight down the steep hill through the woods to a farm gate on the other side of which is either deep track marks when dry or boggy ground when wet. Head for the opening on the other side of the field directly opposite and turn left, onto another rough track with the Burn of Coire Seileach on your right.

The walk along this track is short leading to more gates taking you across the burn via well-maintained steps but before descending to the burn take in the view, these being the hills to your front and above, called collectively the hills of Cromdale. The one on the right being the second highest at 710m, called Carn a Ghillie Chearr. These are not the wildest of hills in the area but certainly a good indicator of those lining the River Spey and her tributaries towards their sources.

Across the burn, follow the route markers to the right, which lead to a feature of this part of the route involving you being lead to a narrow path boarded between fields with gates either end. At the top of this, you are taken onto another narrow path between low woodland and a field.

After all the rough ground since leaving the pinewoods, Cyclists are again offered a breather. At the end of this path, a tall gate leads to wide tracks through this low wood leading to the pinewoods once again after another tall gate. From here it is a nice descent over firm gravel, at the junction turn left up a gentle ascent until another tall gate is reached. Turn right here following the high fence around the low woods, where

Photo 47 – View from Burn of Coire Seilcach towards Tom a Chait

views start to open up of above but more importantly of below, giving you an excellent vantage point of the path ahead to the narrow road above Mains of Dalvey . Especially take note of the woodlands below left many of which you will be skirting.

The path down the length of the field is at first very firm although can be rough more so after the farm gate when the path is narrow again and starts to take on a very boggy feel. This is most evident at the bottom after you turn left following the line of woods where there are slabs of stone again over the wetter areas.

Follow the markers round the woods to a short ascent across a burn, then along a field to farm tracks. Still keeping to the marked trail, your lead along another sparse woodland through a small field bringing you out onto fields with farm tracks running along the fence line. There might be cows and bulls within this large field, just keep to the fenced off part of the walk and off the farm tracks and you will not need to encounter them.

This path leads you up to another farm gate where you turn right heading towards the denser Meiklepark wood. The path here leads you along the length of an old stonewall within the woods where it can get boggy due to the nearby burn and very uneven.

Eventually this path comes out onto a farm track leading you round and down to some farm buildings. Turn left just before these to a small wooden bridge over the Burn of Dalvey then it is a short walk over the field to the narrow road just above Mains of Dalvey.

That last section of the walk is one of the roughest during the whole of this stage over very boggy or stony and uneven ground with many of the guillotine gates between the fenced off sections alongside the woods or across fields. For Cyclists it is very much impossible to use the bike along the last rough part but walkers would have enjoyed the continuous challenge of the change of route, conditions and pace.

Mains of Dalvey to Grantown on Spey

Distance – 7.5 miles   Height gain/loss – 96m/62m

This pace continues for walkers upon joining the narrow road, just walk a short distance down towards the A95 to join the Moray Way along a narrow path up and into the woods of Tom an Uird joining onto the forest tracks within leading to the A95 across the road from Pollowick.

For Cyclists there are two other options, one being to continue down the A95 to the sharp right hand turning into Pollowick (just past the woods on your right). Alternatively, turn left up along this narrow road and take the opportunity to view Cromdale (meaning crooked plain due to the bend in the River Spey) from above within the Haughs of Cromdale and see the Hills of Cromdale above in more detail. Plus this road brings you close to the location of the Battle of Cromdale.

It occurred in the early hours of the 30 April 1690, with the Government forces under Sir Thomas Livingston using aged old tactics against a mighty highland Jacobite force under Major General-Buchan, that of attacking at first light. Back then, rules of encampment may not have included everybody standing too at first and last light, but there were sentries out by the banks of the River Spey by Delachapple. These the Government forces quickly dealt with before the main force of Grants,

Photo 48 – Cromdale Railway Station

Photo 49 – The path within Anagach Woods

and Dragoons made for the Jacobite camp within the Haughs of Cromdale (NJ103277).

Despite a warning being raised by the sentries, the Highlanders were caught totally unawares and despite a gallant stand the proceeding rout rather than a battle did not last long. Some Highlanders did make a stand at the farm of Lethendry but were later taken prisoners while some escaped into an early morning mist.

Apart from a plaque, commemorating the battle a stone can be seen at Clach nam Piobair (NJ104268), called the Pipers Stone. This is in memory of Hamish, the Grants piper whose tunes are said to have given them courage and final victory until he was shot. Legend has it that he appears sometimes with hand out stretched ready to lead you to where he and his comrades lay.

Other Cairns or stones built by the people of Cromdale can be found on the summits above you to the left with the Jubilee Cairn on Creagan a Chaise commemorating the golden jubilee of Queen Victoria in 1887. In addition, the Coronation Cairn celebrating the Coronation of King Edward VII and Queen Alexandria, situated on the top (635m) just above the pipers stone (NJ108260).

If you do venture up onto the hills of Cromdale, in all likelihood you will be doing so along a path that smugglers once used between here and Glenlivet due to this area profound activity in illicit stills. In fact this whole side of the glen was once dotted with obscure small shelters or caves producing the occasional whiff of smoke, some even just a stone's throw up the Burn of Cromdale from the Balmenach Distillery, one of the first legal distilleries started in 1824 by James Macgregor.

From the Haughs off Cromdale you descend to the small town, turn left onto the A95 and take the path beside the narrow bridge. Once across take the first right leading to the River Spey and another old cast Iron bridge. For those who opted for the lower routes to Pollowick, after turning off the A95, descend the gravel track turning left at the bottom and re join the disused railway track.

The length of it from here to the Station is over farmland where you will encounter many gates that need to be opened over ground that is covered in grass and wet in places. Whatever you do, do not go off it towards the River (which it runs parallel to) due to the recordings in the past of the presence of one of the many superstitious animals, a kelpie horse whose favorite hobby was to entice men onto her back to drown them as she descended into the river. Locally the pool in question is called Poll Nan Craobhan.

If you see a most magnificent horse brimming with beauty and strength, do not go near it. For men they are fatal but women can sometimes charm them into wearing a bridle with a cross on it, thus enslaving it. A good way to tell a normal horse from a Kelpie is to scratch its head, it is said to enjoy this but then again so do most normal horses but if you can see sand or seaweed around it then walk away very quickly.

After safely arriving by the Station, carry on under the bridge and turn right to join the road passing by the old church and over the bridge, which was financed by the locals using War Surplus supplies and erected in 1922.

Across the bridge turn left down the gravel track, then right along a path leading to the boundary gate into the Scots pines of Anagach Woods created around 1766 when Sir James Grant of Grant founded Grantown on Spey. Within the woods, follow the marked trail leading you along wide graveled paths keeping an eye out as you go for red squirrels performing their acrobatics on the pines and Roe Deer within the clearings, plus Capercaillie whose early morning courting antics can be witnessed in spring. But most importantly, enjoy the silence and ancient scenery with the smell of pine and forest floor of needles and heather with a few Bilberry bushes dotted around carrying their small dark round nutritious berries towards late summer.

By the exit of the wood are information boards giving more information about the wood. From there turn right heading towards the centre of town, turning right and immediately left at the junction where your led to the town square. From here, you can shop or eat, and as for accommodation, there is plenty of B and B's, with Brooklyn House on Grant Road able to offer parking for Bikes. If camping is more your style then cross over the main road and head up the road to the left of the Coop which will lead you to the campsite.

To continue along the Moray Way, carry on along the road beside the campsite, under the bridge and right up to the disused railway track.

Stage 7 – Grantown on Spey to Dava – OS sheet 36, 27, 419, 418

Distance – 8.4 miles   Height gain/loss – 106m/30m

'Stand Fast Craigellachie!

The defiant call of the Clan Grant, whose rule spanned from Craigellachie to the east and the Crag of Craigellachie above Aviemore to the west.

With fires alight and burning on these borders of stone, the highlanders came running for war as gentleman of honour on a word of trust.'

To the lowlander, the grower of seeds, the tiller of land and fisherman of sea, the hoarder of wealth, they think not a lot,

But fellow highlanders, fighters of freedom, dwellers on the heather at night, with high spirits and energy, they regard as gentleman by Claymore and hand shake.

Times long past during clan feuds, the highlander unlike the wealthy lowlander of Moray suffered lean and hard times, living much like the mafia within families whose power was hard faught for from other clans and the English government. Some they lost, some they won by shield, mace and claymore or compromise. Other times they raided the rich merchant towns within the Laich o' Moray and later paid rent to their lairds from the proceeds of illicit Whisky. The last great sufferance was the highland clearance when many were sent by force to the new towns of Moray and especially the four corners of the known world. Many died but those who survived found a freedom like no other enabling them to mould these lands into their dreams with only their hands and strong backs. These days, nothing makes a Scot more proud than knowing he is from highland stock.

The Grants came to this area from Invernesshire, ousting the Comyns, turning their residence into a castle over the proceeding centuries, and filled it with relics and memoirs of the many conflicts they were involved in during that time. As well as the castle, a small village developed outside the castle where local people felt safe called 'Freuchie'. By 1760, the village had grown expansionary and the Grants sought the right to build a township.

To help promote this new town being built 2 miles from the castle, an advertisement was placed to attract all or any early entrepreneurs boasting about the areas availability of materials for making yarn or linen (an important business in Moray at the time) plus merchants and tradesman.

Areas of land were offered for lease or feus (rent paid in money or services/grain as opposed to military service) an offer which saw the first houses lining the high street being built with long narrow gardens where they could grow vegetables and keep live stock. These gardens were later sold off and in their place private houses were built examples of which can be seen down the length of Grant Road.

The town looked a mess during its early years of development as most would and it has had its hard times such as when the business ran out of linen after the rise of the cotton industry in North America but other resources like timber kept it going. These days tourism is its best selling point surrounded by and in view of the mountains and moors making it ideally suited for day trips to all facets and wonders of Moray.

Along this first part of the rail track above the campsite, you are in a cutting and can get some good views over the town if you scramble up the right hand side bank. The ground can be rough here and damp within the higher cuttings but this soon changes to the smooth grass shown in photo 50 after you cross over a vehicle access road. The gradient is as expected for a railway i.e. very gradual and even. This being the prominent character of this stage of the Moray Way all the way from Grantown on Spey to Forres with only a few places going off the rail track onto rough narrow paths.

The first of these is about 30m past the bridge over the A939 and the old but grand buildings underneath it. The path is initially very rough with lots of exposed roots leading to an access road, from here you could just join the A939 and cycle the 100m to the tarmac road on the right just as the main road bends to the left or if you like quaint woodland walks, follow the marked trail alongside the A939.

Follow the tarmac road to just before Lynmore, turning off left into the pine woods, after crossing a fence turn right and before you know it,

Photo 50 – Rail track just beyond Grantown on Spey

Photo 51 – Rail track beyond bridge over A939

your back onto the rail track surrounded by huge bushes of Gorse and Broom. For most of the year, they look like a bunch of drab brown smooth and spiky sticks but in July/August, you will be walking through a sea of yellows. The cause of this abundance of Gorse alongside Broom could very well be a hangover from when they were both harvested and used to make cattle/horse fodder, both can be used to make brooms and the flowers of broom are edible straight from the plant.

Along this part of the track, the gorse can droop over the track as well as that other spiky menace, the nettle, so you should take care if the weather has allowed the wearing of shorts. Salvation soon comes past a farm gate taking you over a short expanse of grass fields until you enter the woods again with the track changing to exposed roots and damp.

A short distance into the woods you will come to a path crossing the track going to Huntly's cave. This is well worth a visit if weather permits to a deep gorge which on this side of it is of shear exposed rock where you may hear and see the activities of climbing groups, if not then the clearly just through the birch trees from the track is a good resting place. The cave in question is on the other side of the gorge, which is more grass and tree covered so called Huntly's cave after Lewis Gordon, 3rd marquis of Huntly hiding there for a while around 1640. Legend also states that it was a lover's hideout before that for a Grant lad and his Macgregor lass and their retinue on the night before they sacked the castle of the Comyn chief, taking his head as a trophy.

From this junction, the track closes in on you as it steepens slightly and the ground underfoot becomes more boggy and damp. The occasional pine over the track helps little and as you near the point at which the woods end and the moor begins it feels like coming out of a tunnel into wide open sea of heather which is the Dava Moor. This is the only place along the Moray Way where you witness the last gallant stand of the pines and woodland against the forces of nature, standing in a long line of defence, beyond this point being no-pine land (except for a few Birch, Rowan and dwarf Pines).

Dava Moor at most times is a bleak desolate place of low sweeping hills covered by heather hiding multitudes of wet boggy areas. Howling winds often rip across it bringing in low clouds and rain, making it in essence the perfect natural motte of defence for the lowlanders. A road and this

Photo 52 – Rough path from rail track

Photo 53 – Woodland just before rejoining rail track

rail track do wind their way over it these days but it still feels as lonely and foreboding as it has always been.

For the Animals and birds, which call this place home, it must be a never-ending uphill struggle against survival, except perhaps during July and August. The winds still howl over and the rain falls in sheets, but it is harvest time when the usual drab browns of the moor turn into a sea of light and dark purples of Bell heather buds and the berries of Bilberry bushes. Whose sweet small fruit make excellent jam and could well be eaten raw offering the same as the wood sorrel known in the highlands as 'Greim Saighdeir or a 'Soldiers mouthful'.

The Bell heather runs deep within the spirit of the Scots existing knee deep throughout the land as grass does in England. There are songs and poems about it, old lost recipes talk of strong beverages made from it by the early ancestors of the land and stories good and bad are told of it round campfires. Of the purple colours coming from the bloodshed by countless battles during Pictish times signifying that it is in continuous mourning for the dead. And the rare white heather, a bringer of happiness to whoever sets eyes on it created by the tears from the lover of a slaughter hero, she shed them in grief proclaiming 'may the white heather, symbol of my sorrow, bring good fortune to all who find it'.

Upon entering the moor after crossing the farm gate, the path is narrow as shown in photo 55 taking you past the small pines and bushes growing along the tracks verges, lasting until the approach to the summit. It is not a notable summit in fact unless a sign marked it you may not even think it was the top as the gradient is very slight leading to it. There is no aching climb to it and certainly, no steep decline from it and the surrounding vista of the low hills does not give you any hint to the fact that you are now on the highest part of the Moray Way, at 320m (1050 feet).

From the summit the track is very stony and rough for bikes leading down then up again into a small group of tree's, from here the track can get very boggy turning into two ruts running parallel to each other with quite firm but heather and grass covered ridge upon which is best to walk and cycle.

The track continues to the Dava School Plantation changing from wet or damp condition to dry and firm where another detour is encountered around a private dwelling. From here, you can either join the A940 for

Photo 54 – The path to Huntlys Cave

Photo 55 – Entrance to Dava Moor

short distance before rejoining the track via a gravel vehicle road on the right or follow the diversion via a narrow path through low-branched pine trees.

Before the railroad was built, their used to be a pub in this area, which catered to the many tinkers, coaches and wagons which used the Forres to Grantown road. The owner at one time was said to be hot tempered but hospitable and many an argument erupted between him and his guests. One of these brought about 'The Battle of Dava Moor' when during one particular disagreement with his patrons; the owner was set upon by a group of Tinkers bearing down on him with club and shinty (similar to a hockey stick but made from the thick trunks of Gorse). He ran from the inn only to see the many adolescents from the local school coming to his rescue. A scene similar to the western bar fights ensued with the brute determination of the youths winning the day chasing off the battered and bruised tinkers last seen running towards Grantown on Spey.

Dava to Divie Viaduct

Distance – 4.7 miles   Height gain/loss – 0m/100m

Bar fights and disagreements are not uncommon even today but the tale of a ruthless man who lived locally thankfully are. This being the dreaded Wolf of Badenoch who lived in the impregnable castle of Lochindorb built on a little isle in the centre of Loch Lochindorb to the west of Dava.

The castle has a long history of battles and sieges many of which failed due to its thick walls and distance from the loch shore, and it also has its inner secrets like the dungeons of old were captives were punished, worse was the water pit vault, a small dark hole filled with water and topped by an iron gate. The Wolf's use of this started a campaign of blood thirst revenge that gave him his everlasting reputation.

Called Alexander Stewart, the Wolf was both powerful and wealthy owning tracts land and an army of trained soldiers. Amongst some of his neighboring landowners was the church who he resented immensely and sought a means to make such landowners regard him as their overlord. The church did not heel to this and eventually excommunicated the a

Photo 56 - View from summit to patch of woods

Photo 57 - Reverse view after patch of woods towards Cairngorms

Wolf. They notified him of this decision by sending a monk to his castle, who in a fit of rage the wolf cast into the dark watery pit.

It was after this that the Wolf did his worst deed, of gathering his followers and soldiers and descending upon Forres lighting the whole town in a blaze, which nearly saw the end of the old town.

A few weeks later after the rumours and fears were at their worst he descended upon Elgin. For it was the bishop from Elgin cathedral who excommunicated him and upon whom the wolf enacted an orgy of fire and destruction on the cathedral and monks within creating a night where the hunger and thirst of heat and flame knew no bounds leaving in the morning a ruin of rock and stone. The Wolf died soon after this action but not before, he suffered remorse for his bad deeds and sought to do penance. The church allowed this from hence he did good deeds giving his wealth to the church until he was laid to rest at the cathedral of Dunkeld.

As you leave Dava, the track veers round to the right away from the A939, the two separated by the Knock of Braemoray (455m) and you are lead into possibly the most isolated area along the Dava Moor. Any sounds that could be heard before from either the road or wildlife just seem to disappear and apart from a few patches of woodland, the nearby ruins and the cotton grass swaying in the breeze seem your only company.

The appearance or strange tingling feeling you get when something does not seem right would be well suited here, all alone with only the crunching of the stones underfoot. If for any reason this feeling grows worse as you pass the ruin of Auchlochan, do not be alarmed it will probably only signify the arrival of the phantom train which is quite often heard around here and the likely hood of it happening during the day is remote because most sightings seem to be on star lit nights.

If on the other hand you would like to experience seeing a great big steam train descending from the sky and chugging its way past you hovering a few feet off the ground you could do this walk at night or join in with the ghost train walks as advertised on the Dava Way website.

Alternatively, you may wish to cover this part as quickly as possible over gravel track and farm gates until you reach the safety of the woodland coming out the other side to the much safer scenery of grass fields,

Photo 58 – Patches of wood within Moidach More

Photo 59 – Divie Viaduct

sounds of cars, and birds resting on the Divie Viaduct offering grand views of farmland and narrow glens.

Stage 8 - **Divie Viaduct to Forres** – OS sheet 27, 419, 423

Distance – 10.5 miles   Height gain/loss – 0m/169m

The Divie Viaduct was designed by Joseph Mitchell and opened in 1863, the same year the first railroad from Perth to the highlands opened. In total, this is one of 8 viaducts plus over 300 bridges constructed over rivers and roads along the railroads length. The more direct route to Inverness from Perth via Aviemore was not opened until 1898, and is still in use whereas this route like so many others throughout the UK closed in the 1960,s due to the infamous 'Beeching Axe'.

The name Beeching comes from the Author of the report 'The Reshaping of the British Railways', which brought about the 'Axing' of over 4,000 miles of track and 3,000 stations (50% of all stations at the time) in order to reduce loses at a time when road travel for passengers and freight was increasing cheaper.

The length of railroad, which operated over this viaduct, was called the Inverness & Perth Junction Railway. it was not long ago when locals still remembered the sight and smells of smoke puffing along the line by the viaduct, and the noise or hiss of steam plus the blowing of the whistle, memories akin to the film 'The Railway Children'. Of black faced engineers, heads pocking out of the rear of the great iron machines, pleased to have passed the most treacherous part of the line over the Dava moor where sometimes two engines were needed for the gradient from Grantown on Spey and on the moors in winter, wild winds and deep snowdrifts did occasionally trap trains. From the Viaduct, it was down hill to the longest platform of the line at Dunphail and on to Forres.

The viaduct is 477 feet in length consisting of seven arches over the River Divie over 70 feet below, situated just before the river passes through deep gorges carved from its continuous acts of erosion. A characteristic it shares with the River Findhorn into which it flows a few miles downstream just below Randolph's Leap.

If you are lucky enough to venture along some of the Victorian paths which follow the banks of these two wild and picturesque rivers, the pure romance and delight might mislead you to feel that 'Randolph's leap' refers to some lovers quest who being from different warring clans leaped across the river to forever either live or die together. Alas, the leap over the 8-foot chasm of the roaring River Findhorn had nothing to do with lovers and more to do with saving one's skin, and the person who did the leaping was not even called Randolph.

This tale of hatred and lust of land and titles is from a time of uncertainty when to keep one's title and land meant to kill or be killed, when your followers back you to the hilt. A time when the ruined castle of Dunphail was home to the Comyns and Darnaway castle to Randolph (Dunphail castle situated along the Divie a mile below the viaduct and Darnaway on the west bank of the River Findhorn).

For many years, the Comyns were rangers of the Darnaway forest, meaning they had full rights to hunting in the forest, until that is Robert the Bruce gave the earldom of Moray to Randolph. From this time forward, he disregarded the Comyns status as rangers and hunted where he pleased causing the start of a neighborhood dispute between the two.

This dispute come to a head when the Comyns decided to raise their standard throughout their land bringing forth 1000 of their followers with whom they descended upon Darnaway castle. Total surprise would have been achieved if it were not for a spy amongst the Comyns who was able to give warning to Randolph.

Randolph used this information to lay an ambush catching the Comyns totally surprised on the west side of the river where they were driven to under a fierce attack. The ambush was a total success turning the Comyns force into a disorganized army unable to reorganize amongst the thick pinewoods. Eventually the Comyns turned and ran towards the River Findhorn and the safety on their side of the bank. Here their leader threw the clans standard across the river shouting 'Let the Bravest Keep it' after which he leaped across the river vanishing into the forest making for a secret cave along the River Divie with a few of his followers.

The Comyns leader undeterred by the defeat later regrouped his remaining followers and together they stealthily gained access into Randolph's camp posing as peasants. Here they managed to cause such havoc that Randolph pursued them all the way to their cave where he ordered the entrance to be covered with branches and twigs. Once these were set alight, there was no hope for the gallant men inside as they all suffocated to death. Not happy with just killing them, Randolph

Photo 60 – Entrance to the Breathing space

Photo 61 – Across the farmland

cut off all their heads and throw them over the walls of Dunphail castle nearby. The place where this cave is said to be is in a gully called Slaginnan 'The gully of the heads', ½ a mile downstream from Dunphail castle.

The Randolph's held the earldom and rights to hunt in Darnaway forest from 1314 to 1346 a short time due to all of the male heirs being killed in battles. A curt reminder of days when life was short and bitter, with no short cuts or smooth roads, just like the rough gravel track you'll endure on the other side of the viaduct.

This track continues through the woods until you are lead off it along a rough firm path to the breathing space situated next to the Edinkillie Community Centre, by passing a section of the disused track which is constantly damp. The breathing space was created in 2009 to offer walkers and visitors alike an area for picnics, with benches and tables, shelters in bad weather plus short walks through the varied woodland.

After your short breather, the track continues under a low stone bridge and out onto farmland over firm grassy surface for the next few miles. This is a peaceful part of the route in good weather, in bad you will be exposed to the elements, either way the good side is the views you will get of the farmland, the best along the entire route. The down side for Cyclists in particular is the amount of farm gates, which need to be opened and closed. Some sections of it may also be overgrown with the all too common gorse and broom but these are cut back on a yearly basis.

Into the woods once more, you cross over a tarmac road at Clashdhu from where the track narrows to a path becoming progressively rougher and in wet climates, boggier. The path crosses over two small bridges leading you past large clumps of rhododendrons an invasive species, which can be seen all over the UK.

Just before the old two-arched stone bridge a faint path leads down to a big tree growing on the edge of a riverbank, an excellent place to rest awhile before you take the last detour from the disused rail track.

This occurs just beyond the bridge taking you around an area of the old rail route through a cutting meaning that like the stretch before the

Photo 62 – Last gate upon entering woodland

Photo 63 – The narrow path after Clashdhu

breathing space, it is constantly wet. The detour starts with a gentle climb over a muddy track leading to a nice downhill run over gravel. Cyclists will need to go slowly towards the bottom in order to use the gap around the farm gate, it has a ridge within it and at high speed can cause some discomfort.

After the gate turn left just before the house down along a rough muddy path within the woods, take the right path at the bottom with Cyclists ensuring there in a low gear for this short stretch back onto the disuse track involve steep climbs and descents over very stony ground with lots of exposed roots. For hikers and Cyclists also beware that local horse riders use these paths quite often. If during your trip, you fancy doing some horse riding, one of the most well known providers is near here in Rafford (http://www.templestonetrails.com).

The end of this rough path comes with a long sweeping curve to your left, then right leading you to a narrow path between birch on an embankment offering great views over the locality.

From this point, the going is good over firm track straight to Forres and as you near the town, it might not be too surprising to hear from someone the words 'How far is't called Forres'. However, do not mistake it as inpatients of getting somewhere but more likely they are reciting a passage from that famous short play of Shakespeare's entitled by those who believe it cursed with spells of witches 'The Scottish Play'. At the time of him writing it way back in 1603, superstition ran deep and wild in these parts, of tales of strange creatures, of witches with evil spells who were said to be the cause of all discontent, from strange lights in the sky to the failure of crops. An area where most were afraid of their own shadows and especially of those old women down the road who knew far too much about the healing powers of plants.

Shakespeare must have thought this area perfect for one of his tragedies, for not only had one but three royal figures died within Forres around the 10th century due to vengeful or mysterious means. also there is recorded a case where three witches were tried for the murder of King Duncan around 960AD all because a learned doctor could not tell what else could have killed him except for that of witch craft. They were duly tried and sentenced to death, but would it be a slow painful death by fire or drowning within the local River Findhorn. No, it seems that the local

Photo 64 – Stony path

Photo 65 – On embankment

learned men had been busy devising other means of pain and suffering and they had other means of suffering in mind. Thus, the witches were dragged up to Cluny Hill where now resides the three-story 66 foot tower erected in 1806 in memory of Admiral Lord Nelson. Near the edge they were placed into barrels, the tops nailed down and spikes driven through the sides and you have guessed it, they were rolled down the hill.

Just in case there were other women who may feel it is OK to talk to pet cats (black one's being the worse), large boulders were placed where they stopped as a reminder to all of what happens to witches. Only one of these remains to this day situated ironically opposite the Police station along the path of the main high street.

If you feel like a drink after that revelation, there is just off of the track the perfect place as you near Forres, although considering a 21 year old Malt of Dallas Dhu can sell for £200.00 these days it might not be too relaxing. Dallas Dhu Distillery was built in 1899 to fill a gap in the growing demand for single malts used for blending, the high prices of its single malt are due because after 1983 it closed its doors for good until taken over by Historic Scotland turning it into a museum. No whisky is made here anymore and you will not experience the extreme smells of a working distillery on a guided tour but it still has the sampling sessions.

Round the corner from the distillery the Manachy woods comes into view on your right within which are some easy to hard cycle jumps, these jumps being very high and well worth a visit if you have time, just take the path on the right after going under the stone bridge.

Otherwise, carry on along the path leading you up to an estate road (Mannachie Avenue). There is a couple of choices you have from here to get to Sueno Stone, the one on the map provided being the more scenic route. For the more straightforward route turn left, at the T-junction turn right followed by another right at the next junction, right again (or fourth exit) at the large roundabout. Your now on the main high street and Sueno stone is beyond all the shops, the park, the police station and on your left down Findhorn Road.

For the scenic route turn right, follow road as its leads into Mannachie Rise right up to the top, and head between two houses gardens. It almost feels like your venturing over their private property but between the fences is an access path to Loch View. Follow this road down into

Photo 66 – In woods beyond Woodside

Photo 67 – Bridge near Mannachie Woods

Sanquahar Road past the picturesque Sanquahar Loch on your right where you might be lucky enough to see swans. Carry along this road past the schools turning right at the T-junction, then the second exit on the roundabout onto South Street (B9010). This will take you to Grant Park with the avenue of trees leading to the path up the hill to Nelson Tower. At the T-junction turn right (after buying an award winning pie from the butchers on your left) and the turning into Findhorn road and Sueno Stone is less than a Kilometer away.

Photo 68 –Califer Viewpoint NJ084572 accessible from the B9010 to Rafford out of Forres

THE BEN MACDUI TRAIL – An introduction

It is nice to romanticize about the Scottish Highlands, its huge areas of natural beauty, the lone stag deer on the ridge, clear skies allowing 360-degree panoramic views of distant mountains. The hordes of Midges dive bombing while you are trying to cook the wayfayrer meal....such grand memories!

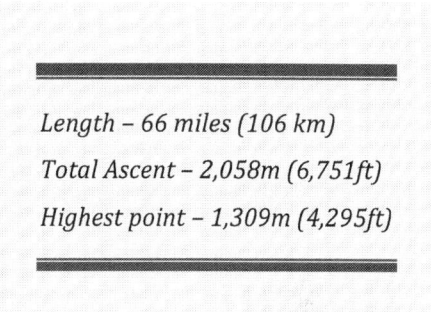

Length – 66 miles (106 km)

Total Ascent – 2,058m (6,751ft)

Highest point – 1,309m (4,295ft)

The Ben Macdui trail, an unofficial route devised by the author is over 60 miles going from coast to clouds. Providing an opportunity to see another side to Moray starting at the old settlement of Burghead, then via narrow roads and tracks over the fertile flatlands or more commonly referred to as 'Laich o' Moray' to the counties capital of Elgin.

From there you really start to venture off the beaten track following the old Mannoch Road, much used in the past by the lassies bringing their illicit gains to market. After a short dip down to the River Spey and a trip to Glenlivet Distillery, the trail continues over isolated moorland into Glenlivet where once hundreds of tiny shelters produced the Peatreek (same as moonshine) as your lead to the high village of Tomintoul.

From there your guide is the River Avon as it leads you through the eerie glen, a river of completely different character to that of the River Spey or River Findhorn. There are no hordes of anglers here or busy roads; it is just you (plus whoever is with you), the sheep, the gentle ripples of the river and whatever Mother Nature is chucking at you.

Once past the last remnant of civilization at Inchrory, the trail and river take on a more sinister stance as a prelude to the mass that is Cairngorms, which after countless twists and turns along the ever-narrowing Glen Avon finally comes into view. Bold, stark and just waiting for you to try to summit it!

Have fun and good luck.

THE BEN MACDUI TRAIL – The Basics

Stage 1 – Burghead to College of Roseisle – OS sheet 28, 423

Distance – 3.3 miles   Height gain/loss – 2m/0m

By bike -   By foot -

Route – From the Pictish Fort follow main road down to turning on right for Beach Caravan Park, turn left and gain access to sandy overgrown path leading to rail tracks, follow these until old wooden structure and gain path up steep bank. This leads to sandy track, which follows the rail track; take first left leading to firm path, and then right onto gravel track and left at junction, which leads to B9089. Turn right onto road, take first grassy track on left to crossroads turn right and follow to College of Roseisle. Towards the end leads to a narrow path round a house, alternative is to turn left off track before this to B9013.

College of Roseisle to Elgin

Distance – 6.5 miles   Height gain/loss – 69m/55m

By bike -   By foot -

Route – At Crossroads turn North North East follow road to NJ156669 and take over grown track between fields to farm track past woods onto road, follow national cycle route 1 signs up to Quarry woods. At road junction turn right then left at NJ184643 up faint path up and over hill down to road leading into Elgin

Alternative routes/short cuts – For Cyclists turn left at junction at quarry woods and follow cycle route signs.

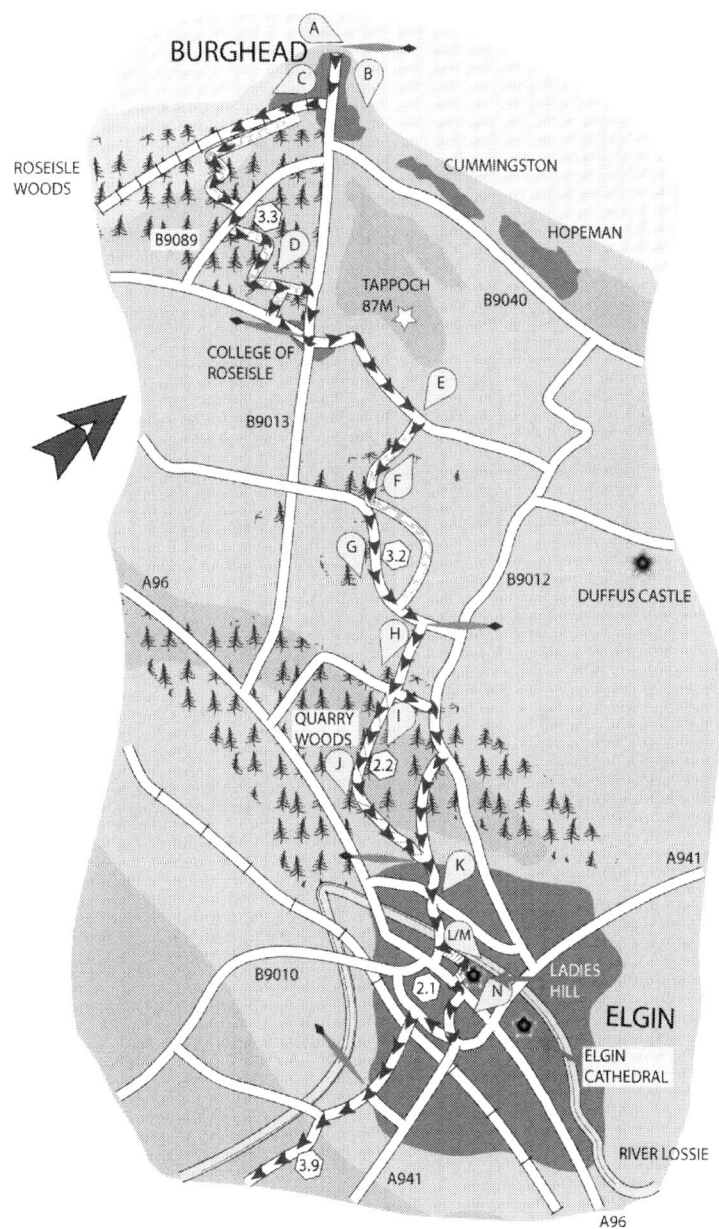

Stage 1 - Burghead to Elgin

Stage 2 – **Elgin to Knockando** – OS sheet 28, 423, 419

Distance – 19.6 miles   Height gain/loss – 276m/172m

By bike -   By foot -

Route – Starting at NJ217611 follow road out of Elgin in a constant Southern direction towards Thomshill getting gradually steeper past to Bardonside leading to track. Veer off left as main track goes to wind farm follow track to lone pine up and over hill turn right at first junction, then left and left again (photo U) leads to boggy moorland onto rough track leading to Mannoch cottage. Cross road follow track past houses and church to B9102, take road opposite to Knockando Distillery.

Alternative routes/short cuts – No alternative but beware section on Mannoch Road between NJ204471 and NJ212483 is constant bog and use photo U to find turning as gap between trees is very narrow and could be missed.

Knockando to Cragganmore

Distance – 3.4 miles   Height gain/loss – 0m/7m

By bike -   By foot -

Route – From road join Moray way on left leading directly to Cragganmore, any climbing is gradual and track is mainly firm but can get over grown and wet. Contains many farm gates but you do not need to dismount to gain access round them. Several wooden bridges and one other narrow one are crossed before gaining the larger bridge across the River Spey into Cragganmore. Gain road from track turn left and follow to A95

Toilets and free camping offered at Cragganmore and at Blackboat.

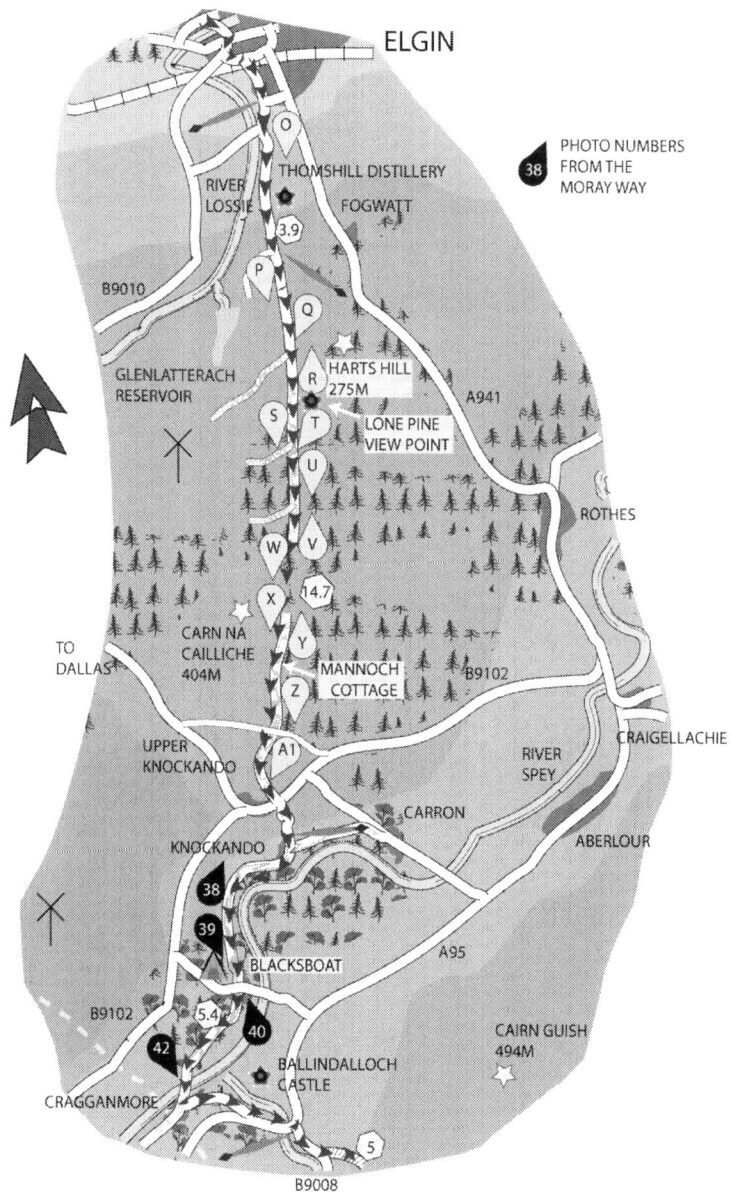

Stage 2 - Elgin to Cragganmo

Stage 3 – **Cragganmore to Glenlivet** – OS sheet 28, 36, 419, 403

Distance – 7 miles   Height gain/loss – 290m/218m

By bike -   By foot -

Route – Follow A95 over River Avon and turn right on sharp bend. Follow B9008 round bend and take first left up steep road, (bins might hide The Speyside Way sign). This leads to a track past a Car park, follow and take right hand narrow boggy path (photo D1). Follow faint path over moors (Spey way signs visible every 100m or so). Near summit veer right then follow fence over boggy and stone path down past farm fields around private house, follow track to road, turn left, then first right over bridge then up track to Glenlivet Distillery.

Alternative routes/short cuts – For Cyclists carry on along the B9008 to Tomintoul or take the B9136 near Drumin castle.

Glenlivet to Tomintoul

Distance – 7.8 miles   Height gain/loss – 328m/218m

By bike -   By foot -

Route – Follow road past distillery, at junction turn right then left onto track which leads to narrow path and follow marked Smugglers Path to Carn Daimh over wet and boggy path. From summit take wide track down to woods, take woodland track on right at junction out onto open moors Follow The Speyside Way signs over moor and through fields, turn left on to road, then right off road through cow field across bridge, turn left over boggy track to A939 into Tomintoul.

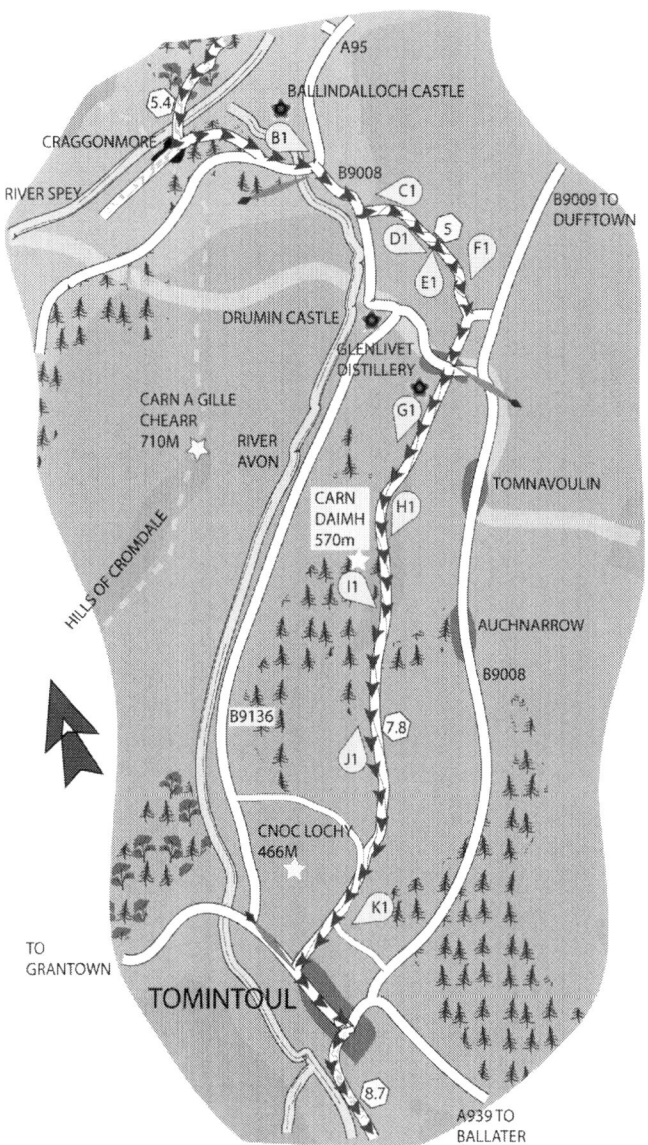

Stage 3 - Cragganmore to Tomintoul

Stage 4 – **Tomintoul to Faindouran Lodge** – OS sheet 36, 404, 403

Distance – 15.7 miles   Height gain/loss – 341m/76m

By bike -   By foot -

Route – Take right hand road signposted to Inchrory at the top of Tomintoul, turn onto track past woods which leads back onto a tarmac road straight to Inchrory (go through big black iron gates) always with River Avon to your right. Past Inchrory take right hand track across river and follow to Lodge over firm gravel track involving steep ascents and descents along the way. Lodge has sleeping room with open fire for cooking etc.

Alternative routes/short cuts – The lodge is as far as a bike can be ridden after which it will have to be carried.

Faindouran Lodge to Ben Macdui

Distance – 9.2 miles   Height gain/loss – 704m/0m

By bike -   By foot -

Route – Boggy, rocky faint path leads from lodge to Ford of Avon shelter. From there follow faint path up to right side of Loch Avon and ascent steep path at NJ010023 and head towards summit at NH999038 where your cross and follow well used path to Lochan Buidhe NH983012 and onto Ben Macdui summit NN989989.

Ben Macdui to Ski Centre

Distance – 4.7 miles   Height gain/loss – 0m/670m

Route – Return back to Lochan Buidhe, take left path towards Cairn Lochan and descent to ski centre or follow track back to summit NH999038 and carry onto NH999039 and descent down ridge to ski centre.

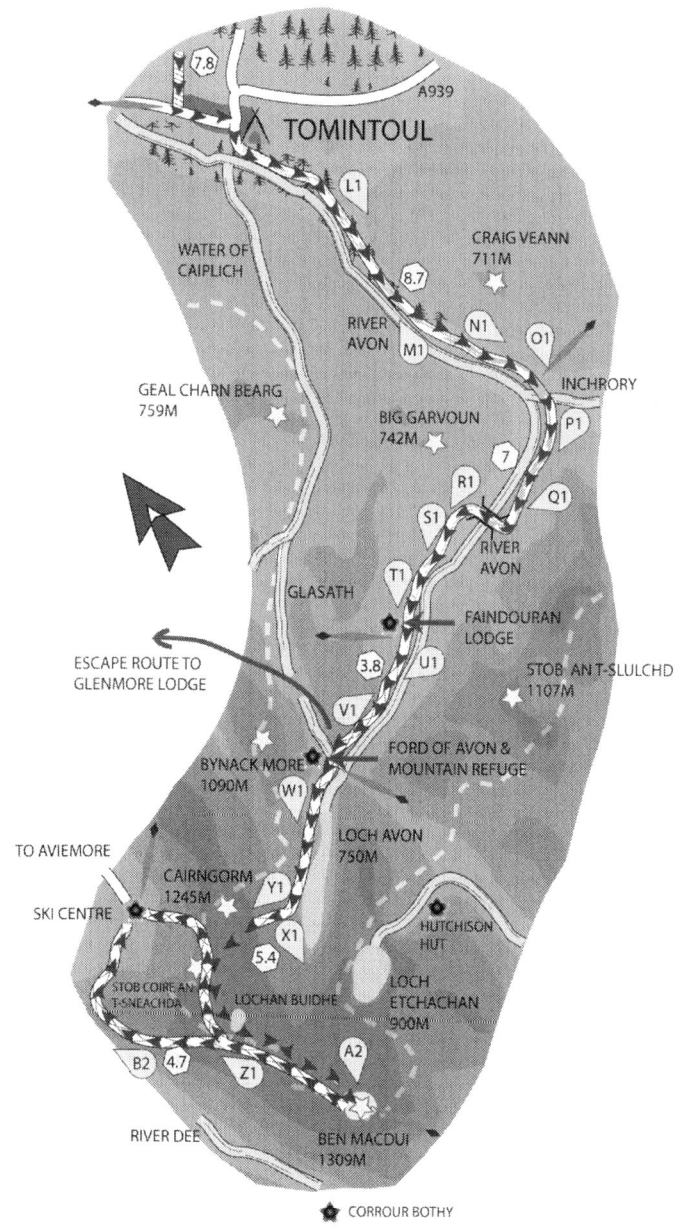

Stage 4 - Tomintoul to Ben Macdui

THE BEN MACDUI TRAIL – The Details

Stage 1 – Burghead to College of Roseisle – OS sheet 28, 423

Distance – 3.3 miles   Height gain/loss – 2m/0m

Burghead is quite possibly the most mysterious and ancient of Morays towns. Not because of its early settlers and the grand Pictish fort, nor even the Roman Well and its disputed beginnings but something that happens for one evening within this town during the dark cold months of winter, whose origins are lost in the murky mists of time. Something kept alive over thousands of years, passed down by each generation.

What is referred to here is of course the 'Burning of the Clavie'. It happens on New Year's Day (according to the old Julian calendar) on the 11th of January when the normally quiet residents perform this pagan ritual to chase away the demands and bring good luck.

The modern Clavie is a whiskey barrel filled with tar and wood, with a specially forged nail made to affix a pole and anchors to the bottom of the barrel after which it is set alight. A group of 15 local men called the 'Clavie crew' led by the elected 'Clavie King', parade the Clavie around the old town, each taking their turn to carry the increasingly burning Clavie just above their heads, while depositing burning embers at various houses and the pubs to bring good luck for the coming year.

The parade ends at Doorie Hill upon one of the few remaining ramparts of the old fort where the burning furnace is placed on an alter. More and more wood is added as the Clavie gradually collapses producing a tongue of fire whose light plays around the surrounding masses, and whose heat beats down and spreads like a cloak chasing away the bad omens. The power of the blasé is further used after the Clavie has turned to ashes when those present collect the remaining embers and take them away as a lucky charm.

When this ritual started, it was held on New Year's Day as according to the Julian calendar, which after the introduction of the Georgians calendar in the 1600 moved it to the 1st of January. In terms of hogmany celebrations, this probably made little difference to the locals or the church of when they drank cordials amounts of Peatreek, but the church did mind the burners of the Clavie performing the ritual in accordance with the Julian Calendar and went as far as rebuking the 'Clavie Crew' in 1689.

Not that it is just the Men of Burghead who have rippled waves, for men have faced each other on battle fields since time began but to face an army of angry house wife's and mums is a different matter, when even a well trained and bloodied squad of soldiers may quake in their boots. This happened during the food riots of 1846 during a bad potato crop at a time when it was the main diet. In its place was grain and meal but the prices of these rose to a degree that put it out of reach of many people, hence the riots in Burghead and its harbour where much of the food arrived. Eventually the soldiers based in nearby Fort George did bring peace, but for awhile some men did fear the stones and broken bottles, which made up the women's arsenal.

As you start the Ben Macdui trail down Grant street stretching before you from the Fort, these opening tales and events will only serve to remind you of Burgheads historic significance as every step you take echo's of many similar tales. After passing the primary school on the left look out for and take the turning on the left down Bridge Street sign posted 'Beach/caravan Park', turn left at the junction onto Station Road. Follow this onto the gravel path where you turn right onto the old route of the railway but it is not until you enter the woods you see and have to walk over the old track still in place. There are other paths within the woods either side of this track, the one on the left being the track you join further along the rail tracks past a broken wooden shelter up over the steep embankments.

This track is wide in places over soft sand, firming up slightly at the point you join it. Take the path, which naturally veers off of it to the left leading to a straight grass covered path between low pines and heather undergrowth. From this point Cyclists should take care within these forest paths as far as College of Roseisle due to their frequent use by local dog walkers and horse riders.

At the cross road of paths turn right onto a gravel path, leading to a wider gravel track where you turn left, this leading you to the B9089. Turn right onto the road and follow for about 100m taking the first gravel track on the left side with the wooden boundary gate. This leads to another crossroads of tracks, you need to turn right here and follow to the end where you are lead via a narrow path round the boundary

Photo A – Museum at the head of Burghead

Photo B – looking down the Grant Street

fence of a private house, into a small stretch of woodland and eventually the road leading into College of Roseisle. Alternatively before reaching the narrow path, take the last wide track on the left taking you to the B9013.

Both of these roads will lead to the crossroads in the centre of the small town, take the road sign posted to Duffus where a small red post box and old red telephone booth can be seen along the line of houses on the right hand side.

College of Roseisle to Elgin

Distance – 6.5 miles   Height gain/loss – 69m/55m

The reason for this little towns unusual name comes from it having at one time during the 6th century a Christian colony and church created here during the time when Columbus travelled from Ireland to this land bringing to life his mothers dream. Of spreading the colour and light of religious teachings like a cloak of immense beauty over the pagan Pictish, people within this region, the centre of his influence being at 'Caer nam brocc' or Burghead.

The college or church does not exist anymore, gone like so many churches and castles of the area and even its location is not certain. It waits patiently under the soil for the archeologist, presently at Clarkly hills nearby to find it.

On your way out of the town, head for Teppoch Hill in front of you and follow the road round to the right. Along this stretch of it is a narrow path on the left between house leading up to Teppoch summit and its ancient cairn. Being adjacent to and higher then Clarkly Hill it offers unique views of Burghead and towards Elgin from where the monks of Roseisle would have seen the Loch of Spynie and Boats rather than the present day view of quiet country roads, patches of woodland and tractors working on farmland.

Carry along the road to grid Reference NJ156669 and take the right hand rough over grown track between fields. After 100m this leads to vehicle tracks through Spindlemuir woods, follow to junction with road at

Photo C – path on left used to depart the rail tracks from

Photo D – Cross road of tracks looking in direction of travel

NJ162658 and carry straight on heading for Loanhead just below Quarry wood, you are now on National Cycle route 1.

Following the Cycle route signs will lead you to Loanhead from where you can once again see the mound upon which the ruins of Duffus castle reside. At the junction above Loanhead, you have two choices of route into Elgin.

For Cyclists, turn left at the junction and follow the cycle route signs taking the well-maintained track at the junction with the B9012 (Duffus Road). This track leads to Brumley Brae, follow to T-junction with Morriston Road.

For walkers turn right at junction and take the faint path on the left into the woods about 100m from the junction. This will lead you in a straight line up to the top of the woods between dense pines on the left and open woodland on the right. It can be rough and muddy but also take you passed some wondrous forest flowers. At the top you may have to walk through dense bracken but from the top the path widens and is firmer via much use by local dog walkers. Follow this straight down, when you start entering Oak Wood and see houses in front of you, take the left hand path just before them leading you to Brumley Brae, and follow the road down to the T-junction with Morriston Road.

From the Junction turn left and immediately right over a narrow bridge down Old Mills Road. You are in Elgin now but this road is very quiet running between two busy entry roads into Elgin allowing you to miss all the traffic and get first hand views of the beautiful River Lossie where along this short stretch to Lady's Hill you might spot Heron, if you are quiet.

After the junction with Jock Inksons Brae on the right, take the narrow path on the left at the end of the tall hedge, this leads you along the river once more. This part of the walk can feel closed in with high stone walls on your right and the over hang of large trees on the left but in sunshine the place can buss with the activities of bees and blossoms, with the old white iron bridge giving access to the open fields beyond. For Lady's Hill stay on this side of the river but do turn up the narrow path between tall walls near the bridge from where it is a short walk to Mary's Well, once the sole source of fresh water for the Castle and Cathedral of Elgin.

Photo E – The rough over grown track between fields

Photo F – Well used track beyond

200 m beyond the bridge, the path veers up between buildings leading to Hill Street. From here, you can see Lady's Hill and the Ruins of the Castle above you, turn right up the steep road from where you can gain access to the ruins at the end of the low wall on your left.

Apart from marking the earliest settlement site of Elgin, the vantage point on top of Lady's Hill will also give you a fantastic view over the whole town allowing you to coordinate your next move, be it to carry on or food and accommodation. The long road you see heading east is Alexandra Road, the best road for these needs, with Tesco's just below you on the left, M and S on the right, plus Halfords further along across the roundabout and lastly the library from where accommodation can be booked. Millets is situated on the second floor of the St Giles Centre accessed from the Bus depot on the right of this road.

What is quite amazing about Lady's Hill is that the remains you see on top of the Hill scattered around the modern monument to George, Duke of Gordon, have nothing to do with the naming of the Hill. The name is from a chapel built on the western side of the hill dedicated to 'Our Lady', which existed there for centuries and was in use years after the Castle had decayed.

The castle was built around the 12th century during the reign of David I. During its time it was seen as the holiday residence for Kings, from where the likes of William I gave court and allowed a mill to be built to the north of Elgin (hence Bishopsmill). Alexander II and III stayed here during many hunting trips into the nearby forests, and of course, Edward I (or longshanks due to his above average height) stayed here in 1296, two years before his huge forces managed to defeat the fiercely loyal and courageous William Wallace at the battle of Falkirk in 1298. The same year as patriotic forces under Andrew de Moray during the Scottish wars of independence attacked the castle leaving it in a state from which it never recovered its former glory despite having been maintained by a succession of Earls of Moray for centuries after.

There are many routes from Lady's Hill to the road junction of Sandy Road and Birnie Road, where you leave Elgin. Which you take will depend on your plans. If those plans are not to stay in Elgin, the shortest route from the Hill is to leave by the south bank down steps to the High Street. Cross over the road heading west posting any letters you may have at the post office. At the roundabout turn up Hay Street (A941), go

Photo G - Cycle route 1

Photo H – Heading towards Quarry Woods

straight over the roundabout and down passed the pedestrian crossing and Moray Street where the police station is. Carry on passed the College on your left turning right into Wards Road just before the Fire Station at the bottom of the hill. Take the first right over the level crossing down The Wards taking you passed an assortment of car garages on your right and Matalan in the retail park towards the end of the road on your left.

At the junction, turn right onto Edgar Road (or left for Asda and B & Q) taking the next left up Glen Moray Drive. Along this road, you will find the last shops and last chance to stock up before leaving Elgin. At the junction turn left onto Springfield Road and immediately right up Sandy Road at the end of which you will gain Birnie Road.

Photo I – Narrow faint path into Quarry Wood

Photo J – Summit of path

Photo K – Narrow Bridge down Old Mills Road

Photo L – Along path towards Iron Bridge

Photo M – Monument on Lady's Hill

Photo N – Looking south from Hill

Stage 2 – **Elgin to Knockando** – OS sheet 28, 423, 419

Distance – 19.6 miles   Height gain/loss – 276m/172m

If you have read the Moray Way details, you will already know that Elgin is not the oldest town in Moray and may wonder why it is the capital of the County when Forres held that honor for so many Centuries. The reason stems back to a time when religion dictated a settlements importance, when this importance also meant the presence of such grand buildings such as churches and centralized trade.

It is not until the second millennium AD when Elgin started to appear regularly in records, specifically about the Castle and the dwellings lined beneath it. Before that, Forres was the jewel in Morays crown. In fact if it were not for Spynie loch drying out and the small Cathedral there being seen as unsuitable for the seat of the bishop of Moray, Elgin may not have gained the motto 'Sic itur ad astra' (this is the way to the stars).

Elgin Cathedral was constructed during the 13th century adding to the Holy Trinity Church already there, over seen by Bishop Richard a favorite of William I whose generosity of gifts and money to the church helped in this new Cathedral gaining consent from the Pope. Thus in July 1224 the Holy Trinity Church became the Cathedral of Moray, known thereafter as the 'Lantern of the North'.

From that time tradesmen and architects of good standing descended upon the town from Europe to revitalize it into a settlement befitting its new status, such as Gregory master mason and Richard the glazier, aided by an army of workers. Together they helped thrust Elgin into the capital of Moray offering a seat of learning and art like no other. The 14th century may have seen its partial destruction by the Wolf of Badenoch but a heartfelt letter of help from the bishop of the time to King Richard II saw it regain its former beauty within a century.

During this time there was an occasion when the town of Elgin was attacked again when the cathedral could have been laid to waste once more. But this time, the bishop and his brethren knowing full well what happened before went out to meet the army as they approached Elgin Cathedral threatening them with excommunication if they proceeded. This threat seemed to steal the fire from their intentions and they relented. To celebrate this victory by the church over wrong doers the

'Little Cross' of Elgin was constructed and can be still seen outside Elgin Library.

For a further 100 years the cathedral grew in importance until the reformation when it started its slow decline to the state seen today which some would say started in 1567 when orders were cleared to strip off all the cathedrals lead. Strong arguments started upon seeing the authorities authorizing the great Cathedrals demolition. Despite the ship carrying this cargo of lead being lost at sea, pleasing those disgusted with its removal in the first place, others felt that it was OK to use the old stone. From then on strong winds and arms slowly brought the great arches and walls down.

In the early 19th century, public outrage finally made the local council create a caretaker to the cathedral, which at the time looked more like something left after bombing. This job was given to an eccentric local shoemaker. For the next 17 years, he, without any government assistance, cleared away the tonnes of brick and debris underneath the cathedral walls while also showing off the surviving grand carvings to those interested. The man was called John Shanks, 66 years old when he first took up a barrel to the cathedral, now buried within the grounds he cleared.

This story brings to memory that of 'Callums Road', about another old man who built a road to his home using only a barrel. Luckily, as you start out of Elgin down the old Mannoch Road to Knockando, you will at least for half of the way have an easy road to travel over, the second half declining to vehicle tracks and total bog in some areas. Still it is not in a bad state considering the construction of it was authorizes by the local council at a cost of three guineas way back in 1792, offering a direct route to the River Spey and Knockando from Elgin. During the early 19th century when Roads all over this area were being improved, the Mannoch was still regarded as an important link between Elgin and the River Spey and only declined in use when the A941 (or its original version) was created providing a safer route within Glen Rothes rather than over the exposed moors.

The history of this road or that of human travel along it goes back far more than just the 18th century. A fact that has recently been brought to light near to the present Glenlossie distillery at Thomshill where single malt has been produced since 1876.

Photo O – The start of the Mannoch Road

Photo P – Beyond the car park near Bardon

As you walk or cycle along this road, take note of the scenery to your right just before descending down to Thomshill. For it was across the field near to the woods where a group of Iron Age settlers made their home comprising of four round houses, the high ground used by their flocks, and the low ground near to the River Lossie where they harvested peat for fires. This settlement like Burghead 9 mile North West from here must have housed an important local leader, for there was not just one, but two large hordes of Romans coins (suggesting repeated visits) found here a total of 300 coins in amongst a treasure trove of other Iron Age finds.

The thought of using a metal detector rather than a walking stick might have crossed your mind due to the hordes at Burghead and Birnie found using them. However, while finds like this are few and far between, finding scenic treasures is more guaranteed especially further along this ancient and rarely used road.

From Thomshill, the road carries on heading directly south towards the narrowing single track as it gets steeper eventually turning into a gravel track beyond Bardon. Follow the signs to a Car park just after the house and through the gate. This rough track leads to a wider gravel track, which is the access road for the Glen Latterach Wind farm, whose windmills can be seen to your right.

The views behind you are starting to get quite breathtaking; if clouds are present, they can really add to the atmosphere of the scenery. This only improves as you travel up the steepest part of this route. Where the wide gravel track splits, take the left hand narrower path heading straight up the hill, after awhile you will start seeing the lone pine bent over to the left indicating the direction of the prominent wind.

Pass by the lone pine, then turn around, and look at the best view along this section. As before, any clouds will only add to the atmosphere of the view. Plus unlike most views, which are confined to a glen or a building, the essence of this view is space and distance. On a clear day, you can see to the coastal mountains of Sutherland across the firth, on a windy day the flowing movement of the clouds above the firth is intoxicating.

Turning back in the direction of travel, you will now fully see the windmills of Glen Latterach Wind farm, whose white surface stands out in sunshine. You will either like this view or hate it. At the moment, this is the only wind farm near to either of the two walks in this book but if

Photo Q – Left hand track leading to Lone Pine, right to wind farm

Photo R – View from the Lone Pine

developers have their way, a farm might also be seen on the Dava Moor in the future

After the lone pine, there is still some climbing to do, but it is very gentle leading you into a pinewood. The track here is firm and rough with the gradient changing to a steep descent after a turning off to the left. At the bottom of the track you exit the woods and enter a wide avenue of grass and heather between two pinewoods coming down from Pikey Hill on your left, the pinewoods closing into it further along where the tracks leads you up again to a junction of tracks marked on the left by a group of young tree's.

This group of tree's is made up of birch and the unusual sight of three Elm's, a rare sight amongst an environment like this one. But they are a fitting start to this section of the walk from here to the ruined Mannoch Cottage, where you will get a feeling, almost palatable to taste, that despite being closed to traffic these days, this old road remembers the woeful steps of travelers past. Whose tree's twisted and rough bark in places wail under strong winds, whose areas of sawn stumps and lone dead trunks left after clearance weep for old friends lost. Where the closed wet marshland of sphagnum, spiny grass and peat await your arrival surrounded by the surreal vision in late spring of snow-white areas of cotton grass amidst an arena of sparse woodland and desert of heather up towards Carn Na Cailliche.

From the three Elms', take the right hand track leading back into the pinewoods and start a short steep ascent to the next junction (photo T). Take the level but slightly over grown left hand track, where after the initial straight section it curves around embankments. The next junction is hard to see due to the gap you need to take being very narrow and over grown, Photo U helps pin point where it is, just to the left through a gap in the embankment as the track your on abruptly turns right up Mannoch hill.

From this point for about 2 miles, the going is very boggy. Once you enter the narrow gap, you will find that the surrounding trees have encroached on the path with some falling over it, but the majority of its length until reaching the edge of the woodland is narrow, wet and covered in grass.

Photo S – track in Pinewoods beyond lone pine

Photo T – First left hand turning above three elms

Out on the moors follow the overgrown track to an old gate. Before descending passed the gate, take this opportunity to look at the track ahead.

Just beyond the small stream below you is the flat area of the marshland, an area best avoided as you will sink into it, you are better off heading for the slight rise to the right of it beating a path through the heather to the far rise beyond the marsh from where you will regain a serviceable track. In addition, start looking to your left as your progress around the marsh, where amidst the sparse pines you might see the dense areas of cotton grass, which from this distance resembles left over snow drifts.

After the marsh the track gradually improves in condition, taking you passed areas of woodland, moors and areas where harvesting of the wood has left the scares of stumps and lone trunks. This eerie section of the track continues along the gentle slopes from the hill above until just after a small quarry where once again you enter into pinewoods.

Follow this rough track down out of the woods; pass the ruin of Mannoch cottage, crossing over the single lane road onto a farm track signifying the end of the Mannoch Road and the lonely moors you have so recently aquatinted yourself with and the start of pastureland continuing down towards Upper Knockando.

Upon entering this little settlement, cross straight over onto the road sign posted 'Knockando Church'. If you want to visit one of the oldest Distilleries in Moray, turn left on the road, which will lead you to the Cardhu Distillery (originally Cardow til 1981).

The distillery got its license in 1824 and was enlarged like others when the railroad arrived, and like them closed between 1917 to 19 due to World War I. The first owners and creators were the renowned Illicit Distillers John and Helen Cummings, Helen being the most acquainted with the Mannoch Road, who is reported to have been a regular traveler along it bare footed taking their liquid refreshment to the eager markets in Elgin. Their first still was at Cardow farm, which also served as the local inn to the surrounding area where even Gaugers stayed during their frequent visits. Upon their arrival, Helen used to raise the alarm to her neighbors by raising a red flag, and disguise her own illicit operation of the smoke and smell by telling them it was her baking. This may have stopped them being caught or their stills seized but in the year

Photo U – Narrow gap below Mannoch Hill

Photo V – Narrow path beyond gap

proceeding John Cummings legitimizing their operation, over 14,000 people were not so lucky.

Before arriving at the church, take the muddy vehicle track on the left opposite the gate of a grand mansion on the right. This leads you down within high trees to the B9102. Cross straight over to and follow the road sign posted 'Knockando Distillery' down towards the old railway station and platforms near River Spey.

Knockando to Cragganmore

Distance – 3.4 miles   Height gain/loss – 0m/7m

This section of the walk follows the route covered by the Carron to Cragganmore section of the Moray way. Please read pages 110 to 114 for full details and photos.

Photo W – Boggy Marsh and slight rise on right

Photo X – Looking towards woodland near small quarry

Photo Y – From beside quarry looking back along track

Photo Z – Beyond Mannoch Cottage Ruin

Photo A1 – Pastureland beyond single lane road

Stage 3 – **Cragganmore to Glenlivet** – OS sheet 28, 36, 419, 403

Distance – 7 miles   Height gain/loss – 290m/218m

This section of the Ben Macdui Trail follows the Tomintoul Spur of the Moray way, taking you up to and over some very fine moorland and mountain environments, places filled with colourful history of battles, not between armies but between the equally laborious illicit distillers and gauger (Tax collector). Their tales amongst a land isolated and untamed cannot be overlooked as the forbearers to the sweet malts of Moray.

So the journey from Cragganmore begins upon turning left from the Moray Way at Cragganmore station starting an ascent on the road to the A 95., Then along the road to the turning down B9008. This short road trip is good for Cyclists, offering only roadside walks for the persons on foot but both should take care due these roads being use by large vehicles and speeding cars. The main attraction along it being the bridge over the River Avon and the old house beyond, get used to the noise and feel of this river (Avon meaning river in Celtic) as beyond Tomintoul it will be your constant companion along the rest of the route to the Cairngorms. For Cyclists who choose to use the roads rather than the rough moor and mountain crossing, it will be your constant companion from now.

Follow the B9008 round the gradual bend and take the first left sign posted 'Auldich', you might miss the Moray Way marker if rubbish bins are out. Cyclists are advised to carry on along the B9008 to Glenlivet, as the path over this moor is very rough.

This side road leads up passed some private houses, at the Car park beyond them carry straight on where the road turns to a vehicle track. Already at this stage you will be getting some grand views back towards the A95, but you are entering exposed hills which might be making the going tough in bad weather. The track continues up into the heather land where it splits. Take the less used right hand path from where the going starts to get wet and boggy. Upon reaching the skyline, you get the first glimpse of an almost endless carpet of heather between the two low hills you're walking under. The path can seem to disappear in places, but the Moray Way markers are positioned every 100m along this part so just keep them in sight.

As you near a sparse group of low trees above and to the right of you, the path you need breaks away from this path to your right appearing well used from the light coloured gravel. A short distance along it you come to the top and get your first inclining of the landscape of Glenlivet.

As you start to descent, you also get to experience the first badly eroded path running along a fence, watch your step here as big holes have been eroded out of the peat and some are well hidden under the dense heather. Follow the path along the fence, if you did bring your bike, the descent after the eroded path is the only area offering firm ground on which to cycle but still watch out for deep boggy areas.

Follow the path over the fence heading towards the Hill of Deskie and rest awhile. Because from here you get an excellent look over the hills of Cromdale to your right, Glenlivet in front of you to the brae's to your left. From here, you are not just looking over great serene scenery but this areas great whiskey heritage.

Whiskey that great elixir of hospitality was first mentioned back in 1494 within the memoirs of King James IV of Scotland. The peat rich streams and rivers below you along with the fertile slopes off the hills where the Bere Barley grew have been used to make the water of life for centuries and still would be if the English had not made it illegal. Even though this started a war of hide and seek, centuries of making and using these illicit gains to help pay rent (in many cases the only way a landowner was paid) acquaint the locals with vast knowledge of the land, and the act of whisky making still went on.

Thus after the new excise act was passed making it illegal to brew whisky (still in force today) many of the highland folk saw it as an affront to their liberties and freedom, not with counting the fact that 'everybody makes whiskey and everybody drinks it'. So thus started the game, many were caught but in the early 19th century those caught were seen as heroes rather than villains. Upon release, they rejoined the hundreds of illicit stills, which existed all around the area you can see from the hilltop. They all used every trick in the book to hide their activities within rough build shelters such as hiding them in deep hollows, caves or near waterfalls to hide sound and smoke. At one point for over 50 years, they ruled these hills.

Photo B1 – Bridge across the River Avon

Photo C1 - Looking back towards A95 from road to Auldich

At the start, the only enforcement the Gaugers had was himself and the law, a brave and brash fellow he must have been to roam amongst these isolated glens. Stories abound of how the whiskey makers fooled them, but what could one man do when confronted by a group of them out in the open but play dumb in order to survive and return another day with an attachment of soldiers.

The surrounding hills are quieter these days. The only fights for survival heard being those of the Red Deer during rutting in Autumn plus the sleek Otter working like cattlemen corralling salmon into pools from where they can take their pick of the choicest. The Glenlivet website (http://www.glenlivetestate.co.uk/index.html) offers wild rides to see these events plus details and maps of walking and cycling routes for the independent minded. Who are not just satisfied with just reading about the area's colourful history but wish to understand how it felt to work in cramped hides with nerves of steel enduring unexpected visits by the Gaugers and thunderous storms.

From the hilltop, a very steep ascent follows the fence down to pasturelands via narrow paths hemmed in from the cattle and sheep by fences either side of you eventually arriving at a private house whose garden you use to skirt around the house to a vehicle track. This track leads to a farm road and eventually the B9008 once again near to a telephone and recycling bins.

Cyclists who used this road route might have taken the B9136 and followed it along the River Avon to Tomintoul. Using this road would enable a short visit to the Drumin castle; a fortified house built on a defence ridge above the River Avon, once home to the Wolf of Badenoch. Further, along this road at Altnaglander starts the white cycle route three offered by the estate allowing access to the summit of Carn Daimh with cycle routes one and two further along the road. The cycle route three can also be reached if you decided to use the B9008 to Tomintoul via Tomnavoulin. More information and maps can be obtained from the website above and are over well-maintained gravel paths most of the time but they can be boggy in places and have stiles along their length.

From the recycling bins, the well-known two arches of the old packhorse bridge is only 200m to the right along the B9008. To carry along the route turn left over the bridge and follow the Moray way signs down a

Photo D1 – Where the tracks split above Auldich

Photo E1 – Looking back at the carpet of heather

rough track further along the road on the right hand side. This leads down to a narrow bridge over the River Livet similar to those along the River Spey. This leads to a gravel track and the single lane road to Glenlivet Distillery. Upon crossing the River Livet, you enter into the Cairngorms National Park.

A fact about whiskey that few may know is that in its original form, it is colourless. For centuries, it was probably more the taste, which pleased rather than the colour, but when this peaty drink started to gain popularity with the English the colour was changed to eliminate its unpopular comparison with gin. Another fact is that after the excise law allowing the legal brewing of whiskey, very few of the illicit distillers took up the offer.

The reason could be that most were happy, as they were, earning all the profits and having few overheads. Some did decide to take the riskier road and gain licenses to produce a product they had had copious amounts of experience producing. The downside was that the cost increased.

One of these included a certain George Smith, shrewed in business both as an illicit and legitimate distiller. One week he was battling the Gaugers and then the next he was battling the hordes of illicit distillers in the area, must have been a very difficult time for him. At least with the law he had some assurance of safety but for some time he had to arm himself against the illicit distillers. So as you travel through the distillery make sure you honor this man's hard work (plus many other since) and take a deep sniff of the angels share.

Glenlivet to Tomintoul

Distance – 7.8 miles   Height gain/loss – 328m/218m

After George Smith's death in 1871, his youngest son, John Gordon Smith took over the distillery enlarging and modernizing it including fitting electric light, years before the majority of Moray had electric fitted in 1965. Apart from carrying on his father's legacy, young Smith was a soldier rising to the rank of Lieutenant Colonel in the 6th volunteer battalion of the Gordon Highlanders. An officer and soldier like many others who, after

Photo F1 – Looking towards the Glenlivet braes

Photo G1 – Entering Blairfindy Moor

leaving, his heart still belonged to the regiment. So much so that after hearing of a siege the Highlanders found themselves trapped within during the Boer war, he sent a cask of the finest Glenlivet malt to warm their hearts and remind them of home. A sentiment that his relative Bill Smith Grant, known as 'The Captain' well remembered during his long association with the distillery and perhaps echoed within one of his favorite statements;

'Give the man a dram, it's like a sweeties to a bairn'

For more information about this old distillery visit their website - http://www.theglenlivet.com/theglenlivet.php - or better still take a guided walk.

After leaving the Distillery, make your way up the steep road to the t-junction near Glenlivet House. Turn right at the junction down the narrow level road taking the rough track on your left and head for the information signs. Your now on the track you would have clearly seen from the vantage point above Glenlivet, heading between two low hills, Carn Ghrataich to the right and Carn Liath the left leading you into Blairfindy Moor.

The track goes down beside a small stream then up and around a ruined building before heading via a fenced in narrow over grown path to the narrow low pass between these hills. A sign near to the small stream points out a rubble of stone and brick further along it within the heather signifying the first location where George Smith started his whiskey-making apprenticeship. The location is certainly isolated, or would have been a few centuries ago, but he couldn't of picked a smaller trickle of water. A good example of all an illicit distiller needed.

The path progresses between two small areas of woodland and a gate beyond which is another information sign of the wilderness you are about to enter. The path starts to take on the characteristics of the moorland i.e. hemmed in by thick heather a fantastic sight when the bell heather is out in full bloom, while the path at first is dry it slowly progresses to wet and boggy with obstacles such as stones and roots near trees. In fine weather, the views to your right of the hills of Cromdale can be fantastic especially with low stormy cloud adding spice and romance portraying

Photo H1 – Junction of paths before ascent to Carn Daimh

Photo I1 – View from Summit west down gravel track

the harshness of this land, if it is raining hard then you are already feeling it.

Once the path levels your lead around the slopes of Carn Liath pass a scattering of low tree's before descending towards a gate. Crossover this and head towards the tree line on your right via a path that is at best described as very boggy which is only 1km from the location at photo H1 but can feel a lot more in bad weather. The junction shown in that photo is of the White cycle route coming from the right out of the woods and walks number 5 'the Carn Daimh circuit' coming from the left, all converging at this point for the steep climb up to the summit just beyond the skyline in the photo.

The top is flat, exposed with only a round platform to hold onto in strong wind on which resides a flat metal plate giving directions and distances to the surrounding peaks. What is best about this summit is the unobstructed 360 degree views from it. There are no ridges or tops higher nearby, it is a statue raising high above the paradise of the surrounding braes, offering a view that matches those of much higher mountains such as the Cairngorms whose distant high ridges are visible through the haze in the distance. From here, it is possible to track the path down to Tomintoul and even the deep gorge beyond into Ailnack. It is all here to see, the deep glen of the River Avon rising up to the shoulder of the hills of Cromdale, the small town of Auchnarrow, and Chapeltown beyond where the braes of Glenlivet rest under the ladder hills. Just make sure the day you visit that the clouds are high, the wind brisk and your boots are waterproof.

From the summit following the wide gravel track to the west, the descent is rough with the odd stone sticking above the rest but for Cyclists a cautious ride down this track is the quickest means to travel. As you near the woodland on your left the wide gravel track veers to the left, those following the white cycle trail should follow it round. For the rest enter the woods via the gate following it up and down to a junction. Turn right onto a level boggy track following it straight out into the open field beyond.

The flowers when in bloom within this field are pleasant to see and serve to take your mind off the fact that unless you knew otherwise you would think you are walking along a stream. This is not an unusual occurrence

Photo J1 – looking back from Croughly towards Carn Daimh

Photo K1 - Direction of travel for the footbridge

along paths in the Highlands whose uses create avenues that the runoff of rain water see as the easiest path to take especially on paths such as this which runs directly down a gentle slope. In dry spells there is no problem but expect the odd pool or two if it has been raining. Relief does occur along it about 100m beyond the side path to Glenconglass in the form of a wooden path built above the wetter parts of this field offering a gentle walk down to Chabet Water and up the other side.

Follow the path uphill using the trail markers as your guide, turning right and then left over the gate and carry on along the edge of the woods, accessing the narrow road via the enclosed path between fields. The exit from this road is shown in photo K1 over a field that may contain cows. If you do not like travelling through cows, carry along the road using the B9008 to reach Tomintoul.

For everybody else, cross the field in the direction shown taking you in the most direct route to the footbridge. After crossing use the steps up to the next field and follow the path alongside the river leading to a track within the Campdalemore woods. Follow this to the A939 and into Tomintoul.

Stage 4 – **Tomintoul to Faindouran Lodge** – OS sheet 36, 404, 403

Distance – 15.7 miles   Height gain/loss – 341m/76m

Tomintoul is another of the planned towns built in Moray and planned by the 4th Duke of Gordon. It was his hope to centralize the highlanders into one productive area to produce linen and yarn but this plan failed. Despite that, after 1780 when the first feus was occupied the town became a resting place for travelers using the old military road the town was planned along becoming a central place to the outlying towns in the 19th century. At a height of 345m above the sea, it is the highest village in Scotland boosting some of the finest whisky bearing waters and isolated wilderness an advantage used well by the many illicit distillers, smugglers and cattle drovers whose trails still exist in the surrounding hills. With most finding plentiful employment from the many Legal distilleries, that sprung up along the many rivers nearby after the excise laws.

If you arrive at the town cold, wet and possibly hungry, then the Old Fire Station Tea Room is the best place to head where their mouth-watering bacon or cheese rolls are just perfect after a hard day out on the hills. While you're enjoying this meal think back to how life must have been like centuries ago when houses were built of mud and stone, the roof thatched with heather and light provided by the local peat ,still harvested today in fields along the B9008. When a walk to the school or Post office might involve 10's of miles and every evening meal was of Potatoes and oatmeal with perhaps some milk, meat being a luxury as deliriously tasty as whisky.

As you look out the café windows, the air might be damp and the clouds overcast but the town's people feel warm to see, quick with a smile and hardy of soul. Summer is their playtime, in winter you might experience some cold back home, here it can cut the outside world out when the town's height and isolation calls for resourceful strength. If you drove here along the A939 from Grantown on Spey or Corgarff, you would have experienced the steep twisting terrain of the roads, lethal in winter and even thrilling in summer when strong winds have turned vehicles over on the approach to the Lecht. Feel lucky then, after a visit to the café and perhaps the whisky castle opposite as you head onto the Cairngorms with a full belly and high spirits, for every day is an adventure around these parts and your heading for the best of them.

Head directly up the Main Street taking the second right hand turning beyond the Youth Hostel sign posted to 'Delnabo'. If you are lucky to be here around early to mid July, you could postpone the trip for a few hours and enjoy the Highland Games, held in a field just along this road.

If not then carry on down the road veering off it within the trees to a gravel track. The small lay by on the left serves as parking for the viewpoint just above you known as the 'Green Gate' most notable for its impressive look out onto the River Avon, as commented by Queen Victoria during one of her trips to the area. Follow the track round and just before it descends, you too will experience this grand view, albeit from a slightly lower vantage point.

Of the River Avon sweeping wide around fertile Haughs from one side of the narrow glen to the other, whose shallow depth creates a vision of soft silk trickling over rocks and a sound of soothing contentment, coursing down a glen bordered with sparsely treed rocky slopes.

Most people's first glimpse of the Cairngorms will be of the north facing ridges and corries from the A9, a vision, which passes as quickly as it appeared. But the appeal and glory of these mountains are not just for pretty postcards. It is the experience and sheer delight of setting foot upon her flanks, seeing how the soft light of sunrise plays like a kaleidoscope over her pink granite and chunks of speckled rock crystal, slowly revealing hidden secrets within the shadows beneath steep cliffs. Of boulder caves big enough to sleep in, of paths made by humans and deer leading over thick clusters of heather up to the dizzy heights of the huge plateau, where on a clear day distant rolling and treeless mountains, cut sheared and rounded by eons of water and ice can be seen.

This then is your destination and this first part of the route over tarmac can deceive the inexperienced of the harsh paths to come, even a gravel track allows for vehicular access to as far as the lodge. Thereafter the characteristic paths of these mountains start; wet, narrow, very rough across steep gradients, and occasionally straight up them. Walking these paths can be bad enough by foot, by bike almost impossible unless carried or left at the lodge and used for a return trip from Ben Macdui to Tomintoul.

The gravel track carries on from the viewpoint, down to the glen floor rising up into woodland once more before re-joining the tarmac road from Delnabo beyond it. This tarmac road not only allows for easy travel

Photo L1 – Looking south down Glen Avon near Torbain

Photo M1 – Looking north down the Glen from Dalestie

until a few hundred metres past Dalestie where gravel takes over again, but also a gratifying release from the rougher trails covered before and those to come. Through vibrant woodlands, passed sweet little waterfalls and an array of highland plants and mosses, all under the cover of the high sided V shaped glen. Round each corner the scene changes the further, you progress towards the Cairngorms, the slopes and floor slowly going from thick heather, sparse woodland and neat grasslands such as at Birchfield where the local Highland games used to be held, to the long straight, almost barrel shaped scree and rocky slopes just beyond Dalestie.

This part of the glen might not look or feel special but to the many families who used to force a living out of this area centuries ago it was. In a time when superstition was rife many tales and legends developed throughout the Cairngorms of events or from certain features with this glen having two. The first is across the river opposite the old building 'Dalestie' at the top of the rise. Clach Bhan is just one of many little specks on the map, an outcrop of little interest unless of course you are a women. Its name derives from Gaelic meaning 'stone' and 'women' and during the 18th century two seats were said to of been carved into the rock where pregnant women from miles around came to site in the hope that these special rocks would ensure them a painless labour and quick delivery.

The Second feature is slightly further down the River just before Foals Crag of two large stones lying on the opposite side of the river, said to mark where Abhainn, also known as Athfhinn the wife of Fionn, the renowned Irish hero, was buried. She was also known as the fair one who also visited Clach Bhan when she was pregnant. The stones are not there anymore but the name of Fingal or Fionn survives in many places within the cairngorms such as the deep corrie of Coire Cach nam Fiann within Glen Geusachan beneath Devils point, which was a traditional hunting ground for them. Or the best known and where you are heading 'The ford of the A'an' or 'Ath nam Fiann (fords of the Fingalians) said to also be where Fionn's wife died while they were out hunting together along. Before her death the river was called Uisge Ban until in his grief, Fionn changed it to A'an.

Beyond Inchrory, the gravel track leads to a vantage point above the cross roads of Glen Avon and Builg, where you are offered a unique view down both of them. At one time during the 17th and 18th centuries,

Photo N1 - Looking south down the Glen under Foals Crag

Photo O1 – View point beyond Inchrory towards Glen Builg

this crossroads saw a lot of traffic from drovers and other less lawful trades a fact that General Wade well understood and why he posted permanent military patrols here for a few years. They lived in bothys along Glen Builg and are said to have recovered over 40 head of stolen cattle within a few days of arrival.

The view in front of you from this vantage point is of the high narrow pass into Glen Avon, from which the river sprouts in a series of grand deep rocky waterfalls. On the left is the outcrop of Carn Fiaclach leading up to the first Munro along this route, Stob Bac an Fhurain (1076m) from which on a clear day, it is said you can see the Moray Firth. You could if you wish, gain this Munro and those further along the ridge to confirm or dispel this theory via a gravel track on the left just before the wooden gate encountered upon starting the rise up to the pass. You can then regain the route via a path from Cnap Leum an Easaich (917m) down to a bridge across the River Avon beside an old metal hut not far from Faindouran lodge. The Authors own test of this theory was during a cloudless hazy day where he only saw as far as the windmill farm above Elgin. A clearer day could reveal more.

After gaining the top of the pass, the gravel track follows the gradient of the surrounding slopes, first descending down to a bridge over which it zig zags up the other side continuing along the Glen up and down as it hugs the slope. Sometimes above the river and often beside it until after the metal hut previously mentioned when the Glen narrows and rocky outcrop force the track around steep sides one side and high cliffs the other.

Gradually the glen floor widens at which point you can see the twin buildings of the lodge further along the track ahead. Unlike other Lodges within the Highlands, do not expect any type of service being available, these two buildings are really bothys offering some shelter from the Cairngorms summer weather and an open fire plus bunks for a warm restful night's sleep. The left hand building is weather proofed but is just an open room floored with pebbles. The right hand building despite being ruinous one end is the best looked after. The walls are plastered, the fire stocked with wood (as long as previous occupants have replaced it) and tables and chairs are provided, as well as a shovel for all those important toilet needs.

Photo P1 – Towards pass

Photo Q1 – Looking from pass to bridge and zig zag on other side

Photo R1 – High above the River

Photo S1 – Towards rocky outcrops above track

Photo T1 – Twin buildings of the Lodge

Photo U1 – Path beyond the lodge

Faindouran Lodge to Ben Macdui

Distance – 9.2 miles   Height gain/loss – 704m/0m

Buildings of one type and another have been around this location for some time before this small Lodge and stables were built around 1870 for the gentry during stalking season. The other type being shealings which at one time were found all over the surrounding glens, including one up Glen Loin where a gamekeeper and his family lived for some time. Considering the weather it has survived these past 140 years it is in quite good condition but this could have been due to the tradesman's from Tomintoul looking after it during its ownership by the Duke of Richmond. In addition, the Glenlivet estate has improved it with caring hands. The only bad element about it could be its popularity and a problem with Poo's, the misplacement of which have already caused a case of food poisoning. So if you need to go, use the shovel.

From the lodge, the track deteriates to a soggy wet path over flat moorland, staying this way until just before the end of the glen where it narrows dramatically between steeps sides and the path meanders up across the slope. This brings you out eventually into the vast expanse of moorland at the crossroads of the Ford of Avon beside the refuge (Refuge renovated August 2011).

Luckily, you do not have to cross the River Avon at this ford, but the steeping stones do provide some means of keeping your feet dry if you need to, except perhaps if the river is in spate where they will be covered. If upon reaching the Loch of Avon you wish to travel along the well used path on the western side, then crossing the river here would be better than trying further up at the beginning of the loch (as shown on the map). The stepping stones there are not as evident even when the river is low, but that would involve striking your own path from the refuge

From the Refuge, follow the path that parallels the river. When you reach the loch edge, the path divides with a well-used one heading for the saddle above and a faint one heading along the shoreline. Given the state of the shoreline path, it might be worth following the path to the saddle, which re-joins the shore path further along the loch and would

Photo V1 – Back toward lodge in narrow end of Glen Avon

Photo W1 – Looking towards the end of Loch Avon

provide a higher perspective (80m) of the awesome view you have along the length of the loch to the dark cliffs at the end.

As you have progressed along this route from Burghead, the viewing opportunities have been numerous, some if not all might have been totally or partially hidden by low clouds. Unfortunately, this is part and parcel of outdoor activities. In regards to the view at the end of the loch, low clouds can actually improve the dark look and feel of it. Whereas on cloudless days the bright light of sunrise shining off the black rocks below Carn Etchachan is nothing less than beautiful, two great examples of where the same place can seem to be a beauty or a beast depending on Mother Nature's moods. Even from this distance, the high cliffs around the end of the loch feel huge and imposing, this sense increasing as you approach these giants along the shore.

When you arrive at the turbulent waters of Allt coire Raibeirt cascading down from the plateau above, you can either take the steep path running parallel to it up to the plateau if you truly want to gain Ben Macdui within Morays county boundaries. Or carry on around the loch past the shelter boulder taking the path up to Loch Etchachan, a grand sight that you will not be able to see following the plateau route nor the steep corries along the final approach to the summit.

If you need to take a gentler approach to Ben Macdui because your either carrying a bike or just want to see the Loch and test the narrow living space under the boulder then take that route as initially the walk up to the plateau along the river is very steep. The path is maintained and has had stones laid along parts of it but in wet weather it can be slippery and certainly no place to carry a bike.

One particular interesting part of the climb up the river is the waterfalls, the best of which is visible as soon as you start the climb. There is also nice flat boulder near to it from where those nice slow motion pictures can be taken, do not forget as well to turn around, it was near this location where photo X1 was taken.

After the waterfall the path leads, you higher above the river and after about a 200m climb the gradient eases upon reaching the lower levels of the plateau. From this point the path splits leading in different directions, you want to follow the river in a North West direction, heading for the top (1131M) above the Fiacaill a Choire Chais ridge. Before reaching this

Photo X1 – From the river towards the head of the Glen

Photo Y1 – Looking up the river

top you will intercept a wide path coming down from the Cairngorm summit on your right, heading towards the ridges above Coire an Sneachda on your left. Turn left onto this, which will lead you to Lochan Buidhe.

The path from now on is gentle with only a slight rise in gradient on the approach to the Summit from Lochan Buidhe. If there is low, thick cloud a constant line of high cairns from the loch will guide you up to the summit. If you are lucky enough to have sparse cloud then the views, which unfold along this path around you, are numerous, especially of the ridge and corries across the great expanse of the Lairig Ghru, of which you get a tantalizing glimpse along the assent to the loch.

For the most part, you will see a vast plateau stretching out before you leading to rounded tops with dark cliffs disappearing into the lower glens. Whose smooth undulating surface may not compare to the rough strenuous approaches of other Munros, but she is a lady worn down by ice, wind and rain over many millennium, creating curves and a character suiting her dignity and charm.

Sometimes you can walk this path with a feeling that you are at a Sunday market, with many people either walking her flanks or chipping away at within her deep corries in winter. Other times you are left feeling very alone. The one constant is the wind, both soft and mellow gently easing the heat of a hot day or strong and fierce driving you to the ground. Cannot forget the cloud, either thick or low cutting visibility down to zero or just above the plateau wrapping you in a warm blanket, but most times its swirls around the peaks like fingers massaging and calming the temper of this lady.

Rain, yes this lady has quite a few showers and not soft one's either but hard large spitting rain creating rivulets all over the plateau most of which are avoided by sticking to the paths. Snow is another frequent visitor in winter and summer, and spring and autumn, almost any time really. However, winter see's the worse when Blizzards can turn the plateau into a no man's land but also a cross country skiers paradise on clear frosty days.

It is after an early fall of heavy snow and strong winds that the weirdest things can be seen on the plateau, that of raised frozen columns of ice. They are not some strange phenomenon like the grey man of Ben

Photo Z1 – Looking back at Loch Buidhe

Photo A2 – Ben Macdui Cairn

Macdui which is merely you reflected onto cloud. These columns are the product of a walker's footstep over deep snow that is left behind after a strong wind blows all the surrounding soft snow away. Of course, in order to see this would involve winter mountaineering and the local Glenmore Lodge is the perfect place to get training, http://www.glenmorelodge.org.uk/.

After Loch Buidhe you have the gratifying feeling that you are near to the end of this route, just a few climbs and dips are between you and conquering the highest point in Moray. Strictly speaking, the boundary line runs from top to top on its way to Ben Macdui meaning that this last path leads you in and out of the county. You could go from top to top but in bad or good weather, it is best to stick to the path ensuring that your footprints follow those of hundreds of others and not give the hardy plants, mosses and lichens something else to try to deal with. Not only that but the path follows the easier gradient and offers just as good views of the plateau across the Lairig Ghru. In addition, before you know it, you are above the last short steep section and the high cairn of the summit beckons you on, or if you approached from Loch Etchachan, the remains of the surveyor hut will.

You have made it, you're at the top. If you must stand atop the cairn like so many others before you and proclaim your prize, you earned it. From beach to peak, you have walked the byways of Moray to stand with all her glory stretching out before you. Not only that, but you have climbed a mountain, a climb which could be compared to life; where you start by looking up at your elders, before starting the long tiring slog to adolescence right up to Middle age until you reach the top. At this point foresight, knowledge and experience can make the difference between you seeing clear skies and great vista under a warm sun or harsh weather and no view. Whereas one is gratifying, the other could be depressing to some but at the end of the day, you are at the same location.

Photo B2 – View beyond the Lairig Ghru

Weather Station on Cairngorm peak during winter

Ben Macdui to Ski Centre

Distance – 4.7 miles   Height gain/loss – 0m/670m

For the return trip, trace your steps back to Loch Buidhe. As you near it you will see two paths, the right being the one you came along earlier and the left leading up and around Cairn Lochan (see photo Z1). Follow the left one.

There is more than just one way to get off the plateau to the ski centre, others being along at the ridge above Fiacaill a Choire Chais. However, this route offers the best opportunity to see the landscape beyond the Lairig Ghru at the top of the raise above the loch to the Chalamain Gap and Lochan an Eilein. Then as you descend the long finger of Miadan Creag an Leth-choin, those steep rocky corries and ridges you walked along the top of earlier come into full glorious view.

The best and saddest part of this route down is as the ski centre comes into view. The last two, or one day, you have walked, crawled, jumped and laughed with companions creating a comradeship that few of the spanking clean tourist by the centre will understand. Therefore, after ascending the last climb above the Allt A'Choire Chais head for the café in the building on your right, and march straight in with muddy feet and smelly armpits and order that cold beer or coffee. It is either that or wait out in the rain for your lift, taxi or bus to Aviemore!

ACCOMMODATION –

Listed below are two places where the Author stayed. For more options on Hotels, B & B's, guesthouse, campsite, please refer to individual tourist information centres.

Brooklynn Guest House - B and B, Grant Road, Grantown on Spey

Brooklynn@woodier.com, 01479 873113

A place to store bikes, nice and quiet and breakfast is plentiful, just great for the day's need of energy.

Argyle Guest House – B and B, 7 Main Street, Tomintoul

Argyleguesthouse@Yahoo.co.uk, 01807 580766

A place to store bikes might even provide a wash down. Breakfast is excellent, Can provide a lunch box at an additional fee. Near to the Old Fire Station Tea Room who make great bacon and cheese rolls and are open until 17.00.

For great local evening meals, bookings need to be made at the Clockhouse Restaurant - 01807 580378.

Elgin Tourist Centre - 01343 562608

Elgin Library,

IV30 1HS

Forres Tourist Centre - 01309 673701

Falconer Museum

Tolbooth Street

IV36 1PH

Grantown-on-spey Tourist Centre - 01479 872242

54 High Street

Grantown on Spey

PH26 3EH

BIBLIOGRAPHY

Banff, Moray and Nairns Lost Railways – Gordon Stanfield

Flora Celtica – William Milliken & Sam Bridgewater

Heavin up the Gear, Fishing communities on the Moray Firth – Banffshire Advertiser and Matt Shortt

Kingston on Spey – George Anderson

Lays and Legends of Moray

Legends of the Cairngorms – Affleck Gray

Lost Moray & Nairn – Brice B.Bishop

Magic Mountains – Rennie McOwan

Moray Firth, Ships and Trade – Ian Hustwick

My Scottish Youth – Sir Robert Bruce Lockhart

Neolithic & Bronze age Scotland – P.J.Ashmore

Old Morayshire Characters – John Gebbie (editor)

On the Trail of the Romans – Raymond Selkirk

People of the Wildcat Country, Tales from Badenoch & Strathspey – Sandra Macpherson

Pictish Warrior – Paul Wagner

Place names Elginshire – D.Matheson

Portrait of the Spey – Francis Thompson

Romans in Moray, the evidence – Ian Keillar

Scottish Animal & Bird Folklore – Malcolm Archibald

Sketches from the traditional history of Burghead – Alex Jeffrey

Tales of the Braes of Glenlivet – Isobel Grant

Tomintoul its Glens and its People – Victor Gaffney

The Findhorn, the River of Beauty – Thomas Henderson & John Cameron

The Folklore of Plants – Margaret Baker

The Moray Book – Donald Omand (editor)

The Pageant of Moray – James B.Ritchie

The Picts, a History – Tim Clarkson

The Secret Still – Gavin D.Smith

The Whiskey Roads of Scotland- Derek Cooper & Fay Godwin

Three Roman Harbours on the Moray Firth – T.C.Bell

Wells and Waterfalls in Moray – Robert Douglas M.A, M.D, D.P.H

INDEX

View of Glenlivet and Cairngorms from Scurran of Merinsh near Ben Rinnes 840M

If you have an odd 2 to 4 hours to spare, a hike up to the summit of Ben Rinnes would be a good idea. It offers a grand 360-degree view over most of Moray including the middle section of the Ben Macdui trail.

Distance is about 6 miles with an ascent of 530m from the lay by at NJ284360 (Landranger 28) and it is just a matter of following the yellow brick road all the way to the top. Well not actually yellow or brick but the coarse wide gravel track looks like it with the odd section of steps over the steeper parts.

Apparently, someone had a wedding on the summit and there are tales of plane crashes plus of the battle of Glenlivet or Balrinnes – visit http://www.friendsofbenrinnes.org.uk/Tales.html for full details of these tales.

View of the Pipers Stone looking towards Cromdale

This is another short 1 to 2 hour walk, which is worthwhile in good weather, especially if you like visiting battle sites. The Author went via Lethendry to this spot after asking at the houses for permission to park (It is a working sheep farm and tractors are constantly used). Alternatively, there is a small lay by near to the farm track at NJ100285 off of the single lane road which would take you pass the battle site.

For those who would also like to see the memorial cairns, take the track above the piper's stone leading straight up the hill. It progresses to multiple boggy paths all the way from the Coronation stone to the Jubilee stone on Creagan a' Chaise but the views from both are fantastic.

From above Lochan nan Gabhar (Ben Avon) towards the coast

The path up to the tops and peaks making up the plateau of Ben Avon starts at NJ177074 over a gravel track changing to a narrow path after a series of small stone walls that look like shooting butts. This path is quite evident as you climb towards East Meur Gorm Craig but after this outcrop, it fades in and out of existence as you make towards Stob Bac an Fhurain. Regardless of this, the going is good over predominantly stony ground where the Author encountered only a few boggy places on the gentle slopes and flats.

It is quite evident by the state of the paths and visible footprints that this area not visited too often by us humans. Due to this, the Author encountered a lot more wildlife as compared to areas of the highlands and Cairngorms which see a lot of human traffic. Numerous birds and grouse filled the skies for most of the day including a golden eagle that the author startled and saw take off from only 15 feet away, a magical sight. Due to the time of year (late September), the coarse sound of Stags rutting filled the plateau and glens, The Author could hear but not see them.

9231456R00130

Printed in Great Britain
by Amazon.co.uk, Ltd.,
Marston Gate.